HINDU DHARMA

BANSI PANDIT

Hindu Temple of San Antonio

18518 Bandera Road, San Antonio, Texas 78023

Published by
B & V Enterprises, Inc.

First Edition   1996
Reprinted   1997

To obtain a copy of this book, or to send your questions,
comments or suggestions, please contact the author at:

B & V Enterprises, Inc.
925 Maryknoll Circle
Glen Ellyn, IL 60137

$9.00, U.S.A.
$13.00, Canada
To order by mail, add $2 for postage and handling.

Library of Congress Catalog Card No. 96-83841
ISBN 0-9634798-3-0

Printed in the United States of America.

Introduction
Hindu Temple of San Antonio (HTSA)

In 1984, a small group of Hindu families, who were holding Sunday group prayers at their homes in order to expose their children to Hindu religion, came up with the idea of starting a temple in San Antonio. After many meetings, this group chose "Hindu Temple of San Antonio" (HTSA) as the name for their future temple. The HTSA was registered as a nonprofit organization in the State of Texas in March, 1984 with the following basic mission:

"Hindu Temple of San Antonio strives to awaken, understand, and promote the knowledge of Sanatana Dharma for individual and universal happiness and peace."

While the search for an ideal location for the temple began, an interim temple, now affectionately called the "Mother Temple", was established at a devotee's residence. This modest facility was made available for worship for the entire community. In the meantime, the permanent location for the temple was chosen on Bandera Road at the scenic hills in Helotes. With immense dedication from the Trustees, volunteers, architects, builders, and community, the HTSA opened its doors at the current location on March 3, 1989.

The HTSA now serves as a central place for worship, weddings, and various other Hindu Samskaras. During the anniversary celebrations, many learned Swamis have visited the temple in the past and blessed the devotees with their discourses on religious and spiritual topics. The HTSA believes in the universality of Hindu Dharma. The highlight of HTSA's activity is the regular Sunday puja from 10:30 a.m. to 12:30 p.m. along with a discourse on the Bhagavad Gita. The temple strongly believes in promoting education of the younger members of our community, who are the future hope to uphold the Hindu Dharma on this land. Towards this goal, the temple conducts Bala Vikas classes for children on a regular basis and emphasizes a wholesome education in the Hindu way of life. This includes classes in Yoga, religious studies, Bhajans, languages, and vegetarian cooking. The Bala Vikas children regularly participate in religious and cultural activities at the temple. A small library has been set up which houses books and audio/video tapes for devotees of all ages.

HTSA is embarking on a project of building a Mahalakshmi Hall (auditorium) which will serve as a permanent facility for holding weddings, receptions, and other cultural activities. This hall will also house the library, meeting rooms and classrooms for Bala Vikas. The HTSA requests your generous support for its ongoing projects.

It is with great pleasure that the HTSA brings out this publication, *Hindu Dharma* by Bansi Pandit, on the occasion of the temple's 8th anniversary celebration. This book is a compendium of Hindu religion and culture organized and presented in a readily comprehensible manner. This will provide a good beginning for reading the author's other more comprehensive book: *The Hindu Mind: Fundamentals of Hindu Religion and Philosophy for All Ages.* Mr. Pandit has kindly arranged this publication at a very generous discount with the publisher in HTSA's name. This book will be particularly helpful to youngsters in providing them with the basics of Hinduism presented in a brief and readily accessible manner. It will also serve as an introduction to Hindu religious studies for those who are interested in learning Hinduism. It is our fervent hope and prayer that you will find this book useful for your own collection and also as a gift for your children and friends.

We thank the following devotees for their generous financial support for sponsoring this book: E. A. Palaniappan of InTech, G. Durairaj, MD PA, Bakthavathsalam Athreya, K. P. Ganeshappa, Vijay N. Koli, V. P. Swaminathan, Ramakrishna Rao, Kedar Chintapalli, Ram C. Tripathi, H. N. Kumara, Bala Vishwanathan, Amar Naik, M. K. Ramadoss, A. L. Kalantri, Rampratap S. Kushwaha, Kirit Gajera, Bala T. Reddy, Venkateshwara Goud, Raghaw Rai, Chaitanya K. Agrawal and Budhi Sagar.

CONTENTS

Chapter 1
What is Hindu Dharma?

Hindu Dharma, popularly called Hinduism, is the religion of over a billion Hindus, who mostly live in India, but have large populations in many other countries. Hindu Dharma is also known as *Vaidika Dharma*, meaning "religion of the Vedas," the ancient Hindu scriptures. The original name of Hindu Dharma is *Sanātana Dharma*, or "universal religion." (See Chapter 12).

Unlike other religions, Hindu Dharma did not originate from a single person, a single book, or at a single point in time. The foundations of this oldest surviving religion were laid by ancient *rishis* (sages), who taught their disciples the eternal principles of life they had discovered through their meditations The *rishis* did not claim authorship of these spiritual principles. Although some names are mentioned in scriptures, nobody knows exactly who these people were or when they lived. Thus Hindu Dharma is essentially a religion of principles rather than persons.

Hindu Dharma is analogous to a fruit tree, with its roots representing the Vedas and the Upanishads, the thick trunk symbolizing the spiritual experiences of numerous sages and saints, its branches representing various theological traditions, and the fruit itself, in different shapes and sizes, symbolizing various sects and subsects.

Although there is no hard and fast line between one period and the next, the evolution of Hindu Dharma may be divided into three periods: the ancient (6500 BCE-1000 AD), the medieval (1000-1800 AD), and the modern (1800 AD to present). The major evolutionary milestones during these periods are summarized in the following table:

7

Date	Activity
- 6500 (minus denotes BCE)	Composition of the early Rig Vedic hymns (according to David Frawley, a Vedic scholar from the US). Current archeological evidence shows that Shiva worship existed in the Indus Valley Civilization in approximately 6000 BCE.[1]
- 5000	Beginning of the Indus Valley Civilization of Harappa and Mohenjo-daro, that climaxed in 3700 BCE and ended in 1500 BCE due to natural causes.
- 4700	Period of Lord Rāma and sage vālmiki.
-3138	The Mahābhārata war took place in 3138 BCE and the Bhagavad Gîtā was recorded during this war.[2] The Vāyu Purāna (a Hindu scripture) states that Lord Krishna entered into *mahāsamādhi* (yogi's conscious exit from the body) 36 years after the war and *Kaliyuga* began on his *mahāsamādhi*.
- 2609	Period of Sage Vishvāmitra, in whose reign a majority of the Vedic hymns were composed. The Yajur and Atharva Vedas were composed around 2400 BCE.
- 2393	King Bhārata, an ancient king and sage (the 44th in the Purānic list of kings and sages) was born. The original name of India is *Bhārat*, after the name of this ancient king.
- 1450	End of narration of the Vedic Samhitās.
- 500 to 200 AD	The Bhagavad Gîtā was compiled between BCE 500-200. Nyāya, Sānkhya, and Brahma Sûtras were recorded, which later gave birth to six popular schools of Hindu philosophy. Buddhism and Jainism also developed during this period.
200 to 750	Final versions of Purānas, Tantras, and other sectarian literature were developed.
750 to 1000	Development of six popular schools of religious thought, establishment of Shankara's Advaita Vedānta, and decline of Buddhism are the main landmarks of this period.
1000 to 1800	This period saw the rise of devotional movements led by Rāmānuja, Ramānanda, Tukarām, Guru Nānak, Surdās, Chaitanya, Mirābai, Tulsî Dās, and many other saints.

Table 1

Modern Hindu Renaissance (1800 AD - Present)

During the domination of India by foreign rule, many social and religious vices appeared in Hindu society in India. There were many leaders of the modern Hindu renaissance including the following saints, scholars, social and religious reformers, who brought the society back into the tradition of Hindu Dharma:

♦ Ram Mohan Roy (1772-1833), a social and religious reformer, and founder of the *Brahmo Samāj*.

♦ Swami Dayānanda (1824-1883), a saint, Vedic scholar, social and religious reformer, and founder of the *Ārya Samāj*.

♦ Mrs. Annie Besant (1847-1933), an Englishwoman, translated and popularized the Bhagavad Gîtā, and established the Hindu College in Banāras, now known as the Banāras Hindu University.

♦ Sri Rāmakrishna (1836-1886), a famous sage of modern times, infused the true spirit of Hindu Dharma into his followers, who came from all walks of life to seek his spiritual help.

♦ Swami Vivekānanda (1863-1902), the beloved disciple of Sri Rāmakrishna, elucidated Hindu Dharma in and outside of India, and introduced the Vedānta philosophy to the West (see Chapter 19).

♦ Sri Āurobindo Ghose (1872-1950), eloquently interpreted the basic concepts of Hindu Dharma, and expounded yoga philosophy for the transformation of human consciousness.

♦ Rabindranāth Tagore (1861-1941), one of the greatest mystical poets of the world, expounded the Upanishadic philosophy through his songs in *Gitānjali* and in many of his other works.

♦ Mahatma Gandhi (1869-1948), extended non-violence, a Hindu cardinal virtue, to social, national, and international affairs.

♦ Ramana Maharshi (1879-1950), another famous sage of modern times, expounded the teachings of Advaita Vedānta to his disciples, who came from all parts of the world to seek his help.

♦ Dr. Sarvepāllî Rādhākrishnan (1888-1975), a philosopher, statesman, and the second President of India, interpreted the classical Hindu philosophy in the context of the modern world through his numerous scholarly works, such as *Hindu View of Life*.

Chapter 2
Hindu View of God, Individual and World

Hindu religious thought is based upon the belief in the Ultimate Reality (*Brahman* of the Upanishads), faith in the reality of the spirit (*ātman*), and faith in the spiritual order of the world. Through their spiritual experiences, the ancient *rishis* (sages) discovered that there are different ways to approach the same goal, catering to different people exhibiting different levels of spiritual development. Enormous diversity is thus an essential feature of the religious life of Hindus.

Hindu View of God

Hindu view of the Ultimate Reality is expressed in the following revelation of the Rig Veda, the oldest Hindu scripture:

> *"Ekam sat vipraha, bahudha vadanti."* [3]
> "Truth is one, the wise call It by various names."

This doctrine recognizes that the Ultimate Reality possesses infinite potential, power and intelligence, and therefore cannot be limited by a single name or form. Thus, Hindus view the Ultimate Reality as having two aspects: impersonal and personal (see Figure 1). The impersonal aspect of the Ultimate Reality is called *Nirguna Brahman* in Hindu scriptures. Nirguna Brahman has no attributes and, as such, is not an object of prayer, but of meditation and knowledge. This aspect of the Ultimate Reality is beyond conception, beyond reasoning and beyond thought.

The personal aspect of the Ultimate Reality is known as *Saguna Brahman*, that is Brahman with attributes. Saguna Brahman is the creator, sustainer and controller of the universe. Saguna Brahman

10

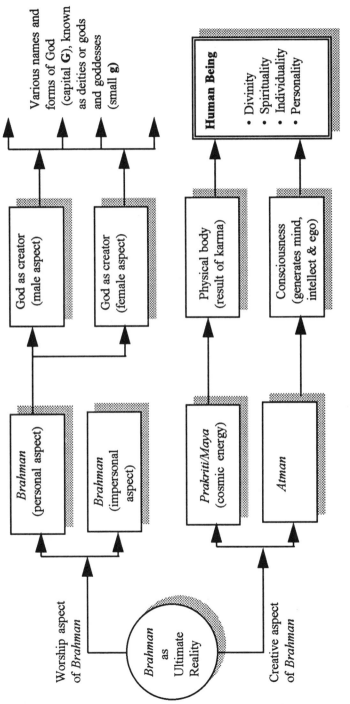

Figure 1

cannot be limited by one form and is therefore worshipped by Hindus in both male and female forms. As the male aspect, Saguna Brahman is called by various Sanskrit names, such as I*shvara, Parameshvara, Paramātma, Maheshvara, and Purusha.* These Sanskrit names represent more or less the same concept as the word God in other religions.

As the female aspect, Hindus refer to Saguna Brahman   by various names, such as Divine Mother, *Durgā* and *Kālī*. Hindus further worship the male and female aspects of Saguna Brahman in many forms, called deities. Refer to Chapter 3 for an understanding of the significance of deity worship.

Hindu View of the Individual

Hindu scriptures teach that an individual is essentially *ātman* clothed in a physical body. The Sanskrit word ātman, meaning "God within," is usually translated as soul, self, or spirit. If the physical body of an individual were compared to a computer, the ātman would represent the electricity that operates the computer. Thus, without ātman, the human body is insentient. In a human body ātman is the source of the mind, intellect and ego sense.

Hindu scriptures declare that ātman is immortal and divine. In Hindu view, therefore, an individual is potentially divine and eternally perfect. There are two states of existence associated with ātman: the bound state and the liberated state. In the bound state, ātman is associated with a physical body. As a result of this association, ātman is subject to *māyā*, which causes it to forget its true divine nature and commit evil deeds in the world. The powers of māyā are two-fold. As cosmic ignorance, māyā deludes the ātman into forgetting its own true nature. As creative energy *(shakti)* of Brahman, māyā is the material cause of the universe. In the liberated state, ātman is said to have attained *moksha* (spiritual perfection) and consequently enjoys union with God. Moksha simply means freedom of the individual from ignorance, i.e. realization of one's own true divine nature, or union with God.

Although there are various viewpoints, the predominant Hindu view is that the same ātman dwells in all beings. Thus, all human beings have a common source and are interconnected in a subtle way.

The reason humans are different from each other (or at least think they are different) is that the manifestation of ātman in a physical body depends upon the type and construction of the physical body. Just as the same electricity manifests as cold in a refrigerator and heat in an oven, the same ātman manifests as a saint in one human body and a sinner in another human body, owing to the past *karma* (see Chapter 6). Thus a sinner of today is a potential saint of tomorrow.

In Hindu view, an individual is not born a sinner, but commits sin due to māyā. Just as darkness quickly disappears upon the appearance of light, an individual's delusion vanishes when he gains self-knowledge. Self-effort and guru's (spiritual preceptor) grace is all that is needed to dispel one's ignorance and attain self-knowledge.

Hindu View of the World

The Sanskrit word for creation is *srishtī*, which means "projecting gross phenomenon from subtle substance." In Hindu view, creation originates from the Ultimate Reality, Brahman.[14] When a potter makes a pot from clay, he makes the process happen and is the efficient cause. The wheel he uses to spin and mold the pot is the instrumental cause, and the clay is the material cause. Unlike Jewish, Christian and other Western theologies, the predominant Hindu view is that Brahman is the efficient cause, the instrumental cause, as well as the material cause of the universe. Thus Brahman is the whole universe, animate and inanimate. With this thought in mind, Hindus worship God as abiding in all created things and beings.

Brahman manifests as consciousness (ātman) and nature (matter) in the phenomenal world. This manifestation is made possible by māyā, the inherent creative energy of Brahman. Hindu scriptures reveal that the manifestation of Brahman as the things and beings of the world is a divine sport (*līlā*). In this eternal sport Brahman manifests in diverse forms in the phenomenal world (creation), stays in that mode for a time (sustenance), and reverts back to the original state (dissolution). This process of creation, sustenance and dissolution is repetitive and occurs in cycles without beginning (*anādi*) and without end (*ananta*). Thus, in Hindu view there is no absolute beginning or end to the universe. Whenever the words "beginning" and "end" appear in Hindu scriptures, they simply mean the beginning and end of a particular cycle of creation.

In the beginning of creation, consciousness is wrapped up in matter. Through the process of evolution, consciousness evolves from lower forms to higher forms of life until it becomes aware of itself in a human body. From that stage onwards, it struggles to free itself from physical limitations (through spiritual discipline) and attain union with Brahman, the original source of consciousness.

In Hindu view, individuals go through the repeated cycles of birth and death, while time goes through the repeated cycles of creation, sustenance, and dissolution. Thus, the Hindu notion of time is cyclic and both time and individuals are viewed as non-unique entities. The Western notion of time is unidirectional and in the Western system both individuals and time are viewed as unique entities.

Practical Significance

The Hindu view of God allows one to exercise complete freedom in worship. A Hindu may worship any deity as he chooses based upon his own mental constitution. He knows that different modes of worship are just different roads to the same destination of union with God. He has no quarrel with other religions as he considers them as different rivers flowing to ultimately merge in the same ocean. As such, he has no urge to forcibly convert other people to his own faith.

The belief in the existence of the all-pervasive Divinity in the universe creates an attitude of acceptance, reverence, benevolence and compassion for all things and beings in the mind of a Hindu. He does not see any intrinsic evil in Nature. He sees the ground, the sky, the trees, the hills and mountains, and the rivers all sacred.

The Hindu concepts of the individual and the world eliminate the fear of God or eternal hell from one's mind. A Hindu considers life a divine pilgrimage from "unreal to real, darkness to light, and death to immortality." [4] Being on this road of pilgrimage, a Hindu has no intention to hurt anyone. He is thoroughly convinced that whatever he does in this life will come back to him in the next life. Thus he must do good and be good now, as he will have to come back again and again in this world until all scores are settled.

Chapter 2

Chapter 3
Why Hindus Worship Deities

Just as a single force in space can be mathematically conceived as having various spatial components, the Supreme Being or God, the personal form of the Ultimate Reality, is conceived by Hindus as having various aspects (see Chapter 2). A Hindu deity (god or goddess; note small g) represents a particular aspect of the Supreme Being. For example, Saraswatî represents the learning and knowledge aspect of the Supreme Being. Thus, if a Hindu wants to pray for acquiring knowledge and understanding, he prays to Saraswatî. Just as sunlight cannot have a separate and independent existence from the sun itself, a Hindu deity does not have a separate and independent existence from the Supreme Being. Thus, Hindu worship of deities is *monotheistic polytheism* and not simple *polytheism*.

Hindus declare that there is only one Supreme Being and He is the God of all religions.[3] There is no "other God." Thus the Biblical Commandment "Thou shalt have no other God before me," really means, "Thou shalt not deny the Ultimate Reality or worship any power other than the Ultimate Reality." (See also Reference 5 in Works Cited.)

Hindus view cosmic activity of the Supreme Being as comprised of three tasks: creation, preservation, and dissolution and recreation. Hindus associate these three cosmic tasks with the three deities, Brahmã, Vishnu and Shiva. Lord Brahmã brings forth the creation and represents the creative principle of the Supreme Being. Lord Vishnu maintains the universe and represents the eternal principle of preservation. Lord Shiva represents the principle of dissolution and recreation. These three deities together form the Hindu Trinity.

One must clearly understand that Brahmã, Vishnu and Shiva are not three independent deities. They represent the same power (the Supreme Being), but in three different aspects. Just as a man may be called a doctor, father or husband based upon the tasks he performs, the Supreme Being is called Brahmã, Vishnu or Shiva when conceived as performing the three different cosmic tasks of creation, preservation, and dissolution/recreation. "The oneness of the three gods Brahmã, Vishnu and Shiva is brought out by the mystic symbol *AUM* (ॐ) where 'A' represents Vishnu, 'U' Shiva and 'M' Brahmã." [6]

Hindu religion is often labeled as a religion of 330 million gods. This misunderstanding arises when people fail to grasp the symbolism of the Hindu pantheon. According to the Hindu scriptures, living beings are not apart from God, since He lives in each and every one of them in the form of ātman (BG 10.39). Thus each living being is a unique manifestation of God. In ancient times it was believed that there were 330 million living beings. This gave rise to the idea of 330 million deities or gods. Actually, this vast number of gods could not have been possibly worshipped, since 330 million names could not have been designed for them. The number *330 million* was simply used to give a symbolic expression to the fundamental Hindu doctrine that God lives in the hearts of all living beings. [11]

"The Hindus have discovered that the absolute can only be realized, or thought of, or stated through the relative, and the images, crosses and crescents are simply so many symbols—so many pegs to hang spiritual ideas on," explained Swami Vivekānanda at the World Parliament of Religions in 1893 (see Chapter 19). A Hindu thus uses a picture or an idol (usually made of metal, wood or clay) to symbolize a deity. The picture or the idol is used as an object of concentration to help concentrate one's mind on the worship, contemplation and meditation. The idol itself is not God, but serves as a symbol of God.

Just as people associate their ideas of infinity with the image of the blue sky or of the sea, or connect their ideas of holiness with the image of a church, a mosque, or a cross, Hindus associate their ideas of holiness, purity, truth, and omnipresence with different images and forms. If somebody were to ask me, "Where is the sky?" I would most probably raise my finger up pointing towards the sky. My finger is not the sky, but it points towards the sky. Similarly, an idol is not God, but a pointer which directs the attention of the devotee towards the Divine.

The whole fabric of Hindu religious thought revolves around the freedom to worship whichever aspect of the Divine one reveres most, based upon one's own mental constitution. This catholicity of Hindu religious outlook is deeply rooted in numerous revelations in Hindu scriptures, such as:

> "In whatever way they [human beings] love Me [God], in the same way they find My love. Various are the ways for them, but in the end they all come to Me." (*Bhagavad Gītā* 4.11)

> "Truth is one, wise call it by various names." (*Rig Veda* 1.164.46)

> "He is the One, the One alone; in Him all deities become One alone." (*Atharva Veda*)

> "Just as the rain water that falls from the sky eventually reaches the ocean, so also the worship offered to Him, by whatever name you wish, or in whatever form you like, ultimately goes to the One (the only One) Ultimate, Infinite Supreme Reality. (Mahābhārata)

The symbolism used in Hindu scriptures expresses the attributes and the qualities of the personal aspect of the Ultimate Reality (*Saguna Brahman*) as conceived by rishis of the yore. Just as a map is used by a traveler as an aid for reaching the destination, symbolism is used by Hindus as an aid in comprehending the Infinite Reality, and for traveling on the spiritual path to the final destination of union with God. The following discussion, based upon the common symbols used in Hindu scriptures, illustrates the symbolism associated with some of the popular deities worshipped in contemporary Hindu religion. Following this discussion is a color plate of each of these deities.

Chapter 3

Lord Ganesha

Lord Ganesha—the Hindu deity in a human form but with the head of an elephant—represents the power of the Supreme Being that removes obstacles and ensures success in human endeavors. For this reason, Hindus worship Ganesha first before beginning any religious, spiritual or worldly activity. In Hindu mythology, Lord Ganesha is the first son of Lord Shiva and the Divine Mother Pārvati. Their second son is Lord Subramanya and their daughter is Jyoti. As explained below, the portrayal of Lord Ganesha as the blend of human and animal parts (see color plate 2) symbolizes the ideals of perfection as conceived by Hindu sages and illustrates some philosophical concepts of profound spiritual significance.

◆ *Elephant head, wide mouth, and large ears:* the large head of an elephant symbolizes wisdom, understanding, and a discriminating intellect that one must possess to attain perfection in life. The wide mouth represents the natural human desire to enjoy life in the world. The large ears signify that a perfect person is the one who possesses a great capacity to listen to others and assimilate ideas.

◆ *The trunk and two tusks with the left tusk broken:* there is no known human instrument that has an operating range as wide as that of an elephant's trunk. It can uproot a tree and yet lift a needle off the ground. Likewise, the human mind must be strong enough to face the ups and downs of the external world and yet delicate enough to explore the subtle realms of the inner world. The two tusks denote the two aspects of the human personality, wisdom and emotion. The right tusk represents wisdom and the left tusk represents emotion. The broken left tusk conveys the idea that one must conquer emotions with wisdom to attain perfection.

◆ *Elephant eyes:* the elephant eyes are said to possess natural deceptiveness that allows them to perceive objects to be bigger than what they really are. Thus the elephant eyes symbolize the idea that even if an individual gets "bigger and bigger" in wealth and wisdom, he should perceive others to be bigger than himself; that is, surrender one's pride and attain humility.

Chapter 3

♦ *The four arms and various objects in the four hands:* the four arms indicate that the Lord is omnipresent and omnipotent. The left side of the body symbolizes emotion and the right side symbolizes reason. An ax in the upper left hand and a lotus in the upper right hand signify that in order to attain spiritual perfection, one should cut worldly attachments and conquer emotions. This enables one to live in the world without being affected by earthly temptations, just as a lotus remains in water but is not affected by it. A tray of Laddûs (a popular snack) near the Lord denotes that He bestows wealth and prosperity upon His devotees. The lower right hand is shown in a blessing pose, which signifies that Ganesha always blesses His devotees.

♦ *A human body with a big belly*: the human body possesses a human heart, which is a symbol of kindness and compassion toward all. Ganesha's body is usually portrayed wearing red and yellow clothes. Yellow symbolizes purity, peace and truthfulness. Red symbolizes the activity in the world. These are the qualities of a perfect person who performs all duties in the world, with purity, peace, and truthfulness. The big belly signifies that a perfect individual must have a large capacity to face all pleasant and unpleasant experiences of the world.

♦ *A mouse sitting near the feet of Ganesha and gazing at the tray of Laddûs:* a mouse symbolizes the ego that can nibble all that is good and noble in a person. A mouse sitting near the feet of Ganesha indicates that a perfect person is one who has conquered his (or her) ego. A mouse gazing at the Laddûs, but not consuming them, denotes that a purified or controlled ego can live in the world without being affected by the worldly temptations. The mouse is also the vehicle of Ganesha, signifying that one must control ego in order for wisdom to shine forth.

♦ *Right foot dangling over the left foot:* as stated above, the left side of the body symbolizes emotion and the right side symbolizes reason and knowledge. The right foot dangling over the left foot illustrates that in order to live a successful life one should utilize knowledge and reason to overcome emotions.

Lord Subramanya - Kãrttikeya

Lord Subramanya symbolizes a perfect individual who has realized the Self (i.e. attained union with God). Hindus worship Lord Subramanya to acquire worldly as well as spiritual prosperity. In mythology, Lord Subramanya, also called by other names such as Kãrttikeya, Murugan, Kumãra, Skanda, and Shanmukha, is the second son of Lord Shiva and Goddess Pãrvati, their other son is Lord Ganesha and their daughter is Jyoti.

In His popular images, Lord Subramanya is depicted in the human form possessing six faces. He holds a spear in His hand. A peacock is shown next to the Lord. This symbolism associated with Lord Subramanya illustrates the following spiritual theme:

♦ Blue color symbolizes infinity. The blue background in the image of the Lord (see color plate 3) denotes that the spiritual essence in all human beings is the Infinite Reality in the form of ãtman.

♦ The six faces of the Lord (for simplicity the color plate shows only one face) signify that the Infinite Reality manifests Itself as God-in-man through the six instruments comprised of the mind and its associated five sense organs—sight, sound, smell, touch and taste.

♦ A spear in the hands of Lord Subramanya symbolizes His power to destroy the enemies of man, such as lust, greed, fear, anger, pride, and hatred.

♦ A peacock feels extremely delighted to see its colorful feathers spread out beautifully when it dances. A blue peacock next to the Lord conveys the idea that man should be very delighted to know that he is essentially ãtman—symbolized by the blue color of the peacock—and is not limited by the body and mind.

♦ Some images show the peacock holding a live snake in its grip. Just as a snake carries poison for its protection, the ego carries the mind for its survival. The peacock holding the snake captive, but not killing it, conveys the idea that man does not have to destroy the ego, but must control it so that its energies can be channeled to discover the Supreme Self.

Chapter 3

Lord Shiva

Lord Shiva represents the aspect of the Supreme Being (Brahman of the Upanishads) that continuously dissolves to recreate in the cyclic process of creation, preservation, dissolution and recreation of the universe. As stated earlier, Lord Shiva is the third member of the Hindu Trinity, the other two being Lord Brahmā and Lord Vishnu.

Owing to His cosmic activity of dissolution and recreation, the words *destroyer* and *destruction* have been erroneously associated with Lord Shiva. This difficulty arises when people fail to grasp the true significance of His cosmic role. The creation sustains itself by a delicate balance between the opposing forces of good and evil. When this balance is disturbed and sustenance of life becomes impossible, Lord Shiva dissolves the universe for creation of the next cycle so that the unliberated souls will have another opportunity to liberate themselves from bondage with the physical world. Thus, Lord Shiva protects the souls from pain and suffering that would be caused by a dysfunctional universe. In analogous cyclic processes, winter is essential for spring to appear and the night is necessary for the morning to follow. To further illustrate, a goldsmith does not destroy gold when he melts old irreparable golden jewelry to create beautiful new ornaments.

Lord Shiva is the Lord of mercy and compassion. He protects devotees from evil forces such as lust, greed, and anger. He grants boons, bestows grace and awakens wisdom in His devotees. The symbolism discussed below (see color plate 4) includes major symbols that are common to all pictures and images of Shiva venerated by Hindus. Since the tasks of Lord Shiva are numerous, He cannot be symbolized in one form. For this reason the images of Shiva vary significantly in their symbolism.

◆ *The unclad body covered with ashes*: the unclad body symbolizes the transcendental aspect of the Lord. Since most things reduce to ashes when burned, ashes symbolize the physical universe. The ashes on the unclad body of the Lord signify that Shiva is the source of the entire universe which emanates from Him, but He transcends the physical phenomena and is not affected by it.

♦ *Matted locks:* Lord Shiva is the Master of yoga. The three matted locks on the head of the Lord convey the idea that integration of the physical, mental and spiritual energies is the ideal of yoga.

♦ *Gangā:* Gangā (river Ganges) is associated with Hindu mythology and is the most sacred river of Hindus. According to tradition, one who bathes in Gangā (revered as Mother Gangā) in accordance with traditional rites and ceremonies on religious occasions in combination with certain astrological events, is freed from sin and attains knowledge, purity and peace. Gangā, symbolically represented on the head of the Lord by a female (Mother Gangā) with a jet of water emanating from her mouth and falling on the ground, signifies that the Lord destroys sin, removes ignorance, and bestows knowledge, purity and peace on the devotees.

♦ *The crescent moon*: is shown on the side of the Lord's head as an ornament, and not as an integral part of His countenance. The waxing and waning phenomenon of the moon symbolizes the time cycle through which creation evolves from the beginning to the end. Since the Lord is the Eternal Reality, He is beyond time. Thus, the crescent moon is only one of His ornaments, and not an integral part of Him.

♦ *Three eyes*: Lord Shiva, also called *Tryambaka Deva* (literally, "three-eyed Lord"), is depicted as having three eyes: the sun is His right eye, the moon the left eye and fire the third eye. The two eyes on the right and left indicate His activity in the physical world. The third eye in the center of the forehead symbolizes spiritual knowledge and power, and is thus called the eye of wisdom or knowledge. Like fire, the powerful gaze of Shiva's third eye annihilates evil, and thus the evil-doers fear His third eye.

♦ *Half-open eyes:* when the Lord opens His eyes, a new cycle of creation emerges and when He closes them, the universe dissolves for creation of the next cycle. The half-open eyes convey the idea that creation is going through cyclic process, with no beginning and no end. Lord Shiva is the Master of Yoga, as He uses His yogic power to project the universe from Himself. The half-open eyes also symbolize His yogic posture.

♦ *Kundalas* **(two ear rings***):* two Kundalas, *Alakshya* (meaning "which cannot be shown by any sign") and *Niranjan* (meaning "which cannot be seen by mortal eyes") in the ears of the Lord signify that He is beyond ordinary perception. Since the kundala in the left ear of the Lord is of the type used by women and the one in His right ear is of the type used by men, these Kundalas also symbolize the Shiva and Shakti (male and female) principle of creation.

♦ *Snake around the neck*: sages have used snakes to symbolize the yogic power of Lord Shiva with which He dissolves and recreates the universe. Like a yogi, a snake hoards nothing, carries nothing, builds nothing, lives on air alone for a long time, and lives in mountains and forests. The venom of a snake, therefore, symbolizes the yogic power.

♦ *A snake (Vasuki Nāga):* is shown curled three times around the neck of the Lord and is looking towards His right side. The three coils of the snake symbolize the past, present and future—time in cycles. The Lord wearing the curled snake like an ornament signifies that creation proceeds in cycles and is time dependent, but the Lord Himself transcends time. The right side of the body symbolizes the human activities based upon knowledge, reason and logic. The snake looking towards the right side of the Lord signifies that the Lord's eternal laws of reason and justice preserve natural order in the universe.

♦ *Rudrāksha necklace:* Rudra is another name of Shiva. *Rudra* also means "strict or uncompromising" and *āksha* means "eye." Rudrāksha necklace worn by the Lord illustrates that He uses His cosmic laws firmly—without compromise—to maintain law and order in the universe. The necklace has 108 beads which symbolize the elements used in the creation of the world.

♦ *Varda Mudrā:* the Lord's right hand is shown in a boon-bestowing and blessing pose. As stated earlier, Lord Shiva annihilates evil, grants boons, bestows grace, destroys ignorance, and awakens wisdom in His devotees.

♦ *Trident (trîsûla)*: a three-pronged trident shown adjacent to the Lord symbolizes His three fundamental powers (*shakti*) of will (*icchã*), action (*kriyã*) and knowledge (*jnãna*). The trident also symbolizes the Lord's power to destroy evil and ignorance.

♦ *Damaru* (drum*)*: a small drum with two sides separated from each other by a thin neck-like structure symbolizes the two utterly dissimilar states of existence, unmanifest and manifest. When a damaru is vibrated, it produces dissimilar sounds which are fused together by resonance to create one sound. The sound thus produced symbolizes *Nãda*, the cosmic sound of AUM (ॐ), which can be heard during deep meditation. According to Hindu scriptures, *Nãda* is the source of creation.

♦ *Kãmandalu:* a water pot (Kãmandalu) made from a dry pumpkin contains nectar and is shown on the ground next to Shiva. The process of making Kãmandalu has deep spiritual significance. A ripe pumpkin is plucked from a plant, its fruit is removed and the shell is cleaned for containing the nectar. In the same way, an individual must break away from attachment to the physical world and clean his inner self of egoistic desires in order to experience the bliss of the Self, symbolized by the nectar in the Kãmandalu.

♦ *Nandi:* the bull is associated with Shiva and is said to be His vehicle. The bull symbolizes both power and ignorance. Lord Shiva's use of the bull as a vehicle conveys the idea that He removes ignorance and bestows power of wisdom on His devotees. The bull is called *Vrisha* in Sanskrit. *Vrisha* also means dharma (righteousness). Thus a bull shown next to Shiva also indicates that He is the eternal companion of righteousness.

♦ *Tiger skin:*. a tiger skin symbolizes potential energy. Lord Shiva, sitting on or wearing a tiger skin, illustrates the idea that He is the source of the creative energy that remains in potential form during the dissolution state of the universe. Of His own Divine Will, the Lord activates the potential form of the creative energy to project the universe in endless cycles.

♦ *Cremation ground:* Shiva sitting in the cremation ground signifies that He is the controller of death in the physical world. Since birth and death are cyclic, controlling one implies controlling the other. Thus, Lord Shiva is revered as the ultimate controller of birth and death in the phenomenal world.

Goddess Durgā

Goddess Durgā represents the power of the Supreme Being that preserves moral order and righteousness in the creation. The Sanskrit word *Durgā* means a fort or a place that is protected and thus difficult to reach. Durgā, also called Divine Mother, protects mankind from evil and misery by destroying evil forces such as selfishness, jealousy, prejudice, hatred, anger, and ego.

The worship of Goddess Durgā is very popular among Hindus. She is also called by many other names, such as Pārvati, Ambikā, and Kālî. In the form of Pārvati, She is known as the divine spouse of Lord Shiva and is the mother of Her two sons, Ganesha and Kārttikeya, and daughter Jyoti. There are many temples dedicated to Durgā's worship in India.

In Her images, Goddess Durgā is shown (see color plate 5) in a female form, wearing red clothes. She has eighteen arms (for simplicity the color plate shows only eight arms), carrying many objects in Her hands. The red color symbolizes action and the red clothes signify that She is always busy destroying evil and protecting mankind from pain and suffering caused by evil forces. Following is the symbolism associated with Goddess Durgā:

♦ A tiger symbolizes unlimited power. Durgā riding a tiger indicates that She possesses unlimited power and uses it to protect virtue and destroy evil. The eighteen arms of Durgā signify that She possesses combined power of the nine incarnations of Lord Vishnu that have appeared on the earth at different times in the past. The tenth incarnation, the Kālkin (a man on a white horse), is still to come. Thus, Goddess Durgā represents a united front of all Divine forces against the negative forces of evil and wickedness.

♦ The sound that emanates from a conch is the sound of the sacred syllable *AUM* (ॐ), which is said to be the sound of creation. A conch in one of the Goddess's hands signifies the ultimate victory of virtue over evil and righteousness over unrighteousness.

♦ Other weapons in the hands of Durgā such as a mace, sword, disc, arrow, and trident convey the idea that one weapon cannot destroy all different kinds of enemies. Different weapons must be used to fight enemies depending upon the circumstances. For example, selfishness must be destroyed by detachment, jealousy by desirelessness, prejudice by self-knowledge, and ego by discrimination.

Goddess Lakshmî

Lakshmî is the Goddess of wealth and prosperity, both material and spiritual. The word "Lakshmî" is derived from the Sanskrit word *Laksme*, meaning "goal." Lakshmî, therefore, represents the goal of life, which includes worldly as well as spiritual prosperity. In Hindu mythology, Goddess Lakshmî, also called Shri, is the divine spouse of Lord Vishnu and provides Him with wealth for the maintenance and preservation of the creation.

In Her images and pictures, Lakshmî is depicted in a female form with four arms and four hands (see color plate 6). She wears red clothes with a golden lining and is standing on a lotus. She has golden coins and lotuses in her hands. Two elephants (some pictures show four) are shown next to the Goddess. This symbolism conveys the following spiritual theme:

♦ The four arms represent the four directions in space and thus symbolize omnipresence and omnipotence of the Goddess. The red color symbolizes activity. The golden lining (embroidery) on Her red dress denotes prosperity. The idea conveyed here is that the Goddess is always busy distributing wealth and prosperity to the devotees. The lotus seat, which Lakshmî is standing upon, signifies that while living in this world, one should enjoy its wealth, but not become obsessed with it. Such a living is analogous to a lotus that grows in water but is not wetted by water.

♦ The four hands represent the four *ends* (see page 55) of human life: *dharma* (righteousness), *kãma* (genuine desires), *artha* (wealth), and *moksha* (liberation from birth and death). The front hands represent the activity in the physical world and the back hands indicate the spiritual activities that lead to spiritual perfection.

♦ Since the right side of the body symbolizes activity, a lotus in the back right hand conveys the idea that one must perform all duties in the world in accordance with dharma. This leads to moksha (liberation), which is symbolized by a lotus in the back left hand of Lakshmî. The golden coins falling on the ground from the front left hand of Lakshmî illustrate that She provides wealth and prosperity to Her devotees. Her front right hand is shown bestowing blessings upon the devotees.

♦ The two elephants standing next to the Goddess symbolize the name and fame associated with worldly wealth. The idea conveyed here is that a true devotee should not earn wealth merely to acquire name and fame or only to satisfy his own material desires, but should share it with others in order to bring happiness to others in addition to himself.

♦ Some pictures show four elephants spraying water from golden vessels onto Goddess Lakshmî. The four elephants represent the four ends of human life as discussed above. The spraying of water denotes activity. The golden vessels denote wisdom and purity. The four elephants spraying water from the golden vessels on the Goddess illustrate the theme that continuous self-effort, in accordance with one's dharma and governed by wisdom and purity, leads to both material and spiritual prosperity.

Goddess Lakshmî is regularly worshipped in home shrines and temples by Her devotees. A special worship is offered to Her annually on the auspicious day of Diwalî, with religious rituals and colorful ceremonies specifically devoted to Her.

Goddess Saraswatî

Saraswatî is the Goddess of learning, knowledge, and wisdom. The Sanskrit word *sara* means "essence" and *swa* means "self." Thus Saraswatî means "the essence of the self." Saraswatî is represented in Hindu mythology as the divine consort of Lord Brahmā, the Creator of the universe. Since knowledge is necessary for creation, Saraswatî symbolizes the creative power of Brahmā. Goddess Saraswatî is worshipped by all persons interested in knowledge, especially students, teachers, scholars, and scientists.

In Her popular images and pictures, Goddess Saraswatî is generally depicted with four arms (some pictures may show only two arms), wearing a white sari and seated on a white lotus (see color plate 7). She holds a book and a rosary in Her rear two hands, while the front two hands are engaged in the playing of a lute (veena). Her right leg is shown slightly pushing against Her left leg. She uses a swan as Her vehicle. There is a peacock by Her side gazing at Her. This symbolism illustrates the following spiritual ideas:

♦ The lotus is a symbol of the Supreme Reality, and a white lotus also denotes supreme knowledge. By sitting on a lotus, Saraswatî signifies that She is Herself rooted in the Supreme Reality, and symbolizes supreme knowledge. The white color symbolizes purity and knowledge. The white sari that the Goddess is wearing denotes that She is the embodiment of pure knowledge.

♦ The four arms denote Her omnipresence and omnipotence. The two front arms indicate Her activity in the physical world and the two back arms signify Her presence in the spiritual world. The four hands represent the four elements of the inner personality. The mind (*manas*) is represented by the front right hand, the intellect (*buddhi*) by the front left hand, the conditioned consciousness (*chitta*) by the rear left hand, and the ego (*ahankāra*) by the rear right hand.

♦ The left side of the body symbolizes the qualities of the heart and the right side symbolizes activities of the mind and intellect. A book in the rear left hand signifies that knowledge acquired must be used with love and kindness to promote prosperity of mankind.

♦ The rosary signifies concentration, meditation, and contemplation, leading to samādhi, or union with God. A rosary in the rear right hand representing ego conveys that true knowledge acquired with love and devotion melts the ego and results in liberation (moksha) of the seeker from the bondage to the physical world.

♦ The Goddess is shown playing a musical instrument that is held in Her front hands, which denote mind and intellect. This symbol conveys that the seeker must tune his mind and intellect in order to live in perfect harmony with the world. Such harmonious living enables the individual to utilize acquired knowledge for the welfare of all mankind.

♦ Two swans are depicted on the left side of the Goddess. A swan is said to have a sensitive beak that enables it to distinguish pure milk from a mixture of milk and water. A swan, therefore, symbolizes the power of discrimination, or the ability to discriminate between right and wrong or good and bad. Saraswatî uses the swan as Her carrier. This indicates that one must acquire and apply knowledge with discrimination for the good of mankind. Knowledge that is dominated by ego can destroy the world.

♦ A peacock is sitting next to Saraswatî and is anxiously waiting to serve as Her vehicle. A peacock depicts unpredictable behavior as its moods can be influenced by the changes in the weather. Saraswatî is using a swan as a vehicle and not the peacock. This signifies that one should overcome fear, indecision, and fickleness in order to acquire true knowledge.

Sîtā, Rāma, Lakshmana and Hanûmān

Lord Rāma is the seventh incarnation of Lord Vishnu. The worship of Lord Rāma is very popular among all Hindus, as is evident by the numerous temples dedicated to him in India. In the temple images, Rāma is usually shown with his faithful wife Sîtā, devoted brother Lakshmana, and his beloved devotee Hanûmān (see color plate 8). The life story of Rāma and the main purpose of his incarnation (to destroy the demon king Rāvana) is described in the great epic Rāmāyana. A study of the epic Rāmāyana reveals the following theme:

♦ Rāma represents an ideal man, as conceived by the Hindu mind. In the story of Rāmāyana, Rāma's personality depicts him as the perfect son, devoted brother, true husband, trusted friend, ideal king, and a noble adversary.

♦ In images and pictures, Rāma is shown carrying a bow and arrow. The bow and arrow convey that Rāma is always ready to destroy evil and protect righteousness. He is himself an embodiment of dharma.

♦ Sîtā symbolizes an ideal daughter, wife, mother, and queen. Whereas Rāma symbolizes standards of perfection that can be conceived in all the facets of a man's life, Mother Sîtā represents all that is great and noble in womanhood. She is revered as an incarnation of Goddess Lakshmî, the divine consort of Lord Vishnu.

♦ Lakshmana symbolizes the ideal of sacrifice. He leaves his young wife behind in the palace and chooses to accompany his brother (Rāma) in exile. He sacrifices the amenities of his personal life to serve his elder brother.

♦ Hanûmān, the great monkey hero, also called Maruti, assists Rāma in his battle with Rāvana to rescue Sîtā, who had been kidnapped by Rāvana. Hanûmān symbolizes the qualities of an ideal devotee of God, which can be represented by the letters of his name, as follows:

        H = Humility and hopefulness (optimism)
        A = Admiration (truthfulness, devotion)
        N = Nobility (sincerity, loyalty, modesty)
        U = Understanding (knowledge)
        M = Mastery over ego (kindness, compassion)
        A = Achievements (strength)
        N = Nishkāma-karma (selfless work in service of God)

After his coronation, following victory in the battle with Rāvana, Rāma distributed gifts to all those who had assisted him in his battle with Rãvana. Turning towards Hanûmãn, Rãma said, "There is nothing I can give you that would match the service you have rendered to me. All I can do is to give you my own self." Upon hearing these words, Hanûmãn stood by Rãma, in all humility, with hands joined together in front of his (Hanûmãn's) mouth, and head slightly bent in the pose of service for Rãma. To this day, this picture of Hanûmãn, as a humble devotee of the Lord, is the most popular among the admirers and worshippers of Hanûmãn.

The worship of Hanûmãn, therefore, symbolizes the worship of the Supreme Lord, for acquiring knowledge, physical and mental strength, truthfulness, sincerity, selflessness, humility, loyalty, and profound devotion to the Lord.

Rãdhã and Krishna

Lord Krishna (see color plate 9) is the eighth and the most popular incarnation of Lord Vishnu. He was born in approximately 3200 BCE in Vrindãvan, where he was brought up by the cowherd family of Yashodã and Nanda. His childhood playmates were gopas (cowherd boys) and gopis (cowherd girls), who were greatly devoted to him. Of all gopis, Rãdhã loved Krishna the most.

In the forests of Vrindãvan, Krishna often played his flute and gopis danced with him in ecstasy. The Gopis represent the individual souls trapped in physical bodies. Rãdhã symbolizes the individual soul that is awakened to the love of God and is absorbed in such love. The sound of Krishna's flute represents the call of the divine for the individual souls.

The gopis' love for Krishna signifies the eternal bond between the individual soul and God. The dance of the gopis and Krishna (*Rãsa Lîlã*) signifies the union of the human and Divine, the dance of the souls. In the forest, the gopis dance with Krishna and are absorbed in their love for him. This illustrates that when an individual soul responds to the call of the Divine, the soul enjoys union with the Lord and becomes absorbed in the divine ecstasy.

Of all the incarnations, Lord Krishna is revered as a full and complete incarnation (*pûrna avatãra*) of Lord Vishnu. He commands love, respect, and adoration from all Hindus of all walks of life.

Chapter 3

Goddess Jyoti

Jyoti means "light" and Goddess Jyoti (see color plate 1) represents the power of the Ultimate Reality (*Brahman*) that illuminates our minds and gives shape and form to all created things and beings of the world.

According to the Taittiriya Upanishad 2.1, the five great elements (*Panchamahābhutas*)—earth, water, fire, air and space—emanate from Brahman.[32] These five elements, together with the omnipresent cosmic consciousness of Brahman, constitute all created things and beings in the universe. In Hindu mythology, this creative process is symbolized by the family of Lord Shiva. The members of this divine family are Lord Shiva, His spouse the Divine Mother, their two sons Ganesha and Skanda, and their daughter Jyoti. Lord Shiva represents the cosmic consciousness, the Divine Mother denotes the creative energy, Ganesha symbolizes the elements of earth and water, Skanda represents the element of fire, and Jyoti symbolizes the two elements of air and space. Since fire uses air and burns in space, in Hindu mythology Jyoti is always associated with Skanda and is known more as Skanda's sister than as Ganesha's sister. She is worshipped in Her formless (*arupa*) aspect in all temples where Lord Skanda is worshipped.

According to Tantra Yoga, Jyoti is the aroused *kundalini shakti* (latent energy) that resides in the a*jna chakra* (energy center between the eyebrows in the forehead) and is experienced as light in deep meditation.[32] In Her popular images, Jyoti is represented as a young girl, dressed in bright clothes. The brightness of Her attire symbolizes the light of knowledge that dispels the darkness of ignorance. Wherever a lamp is lit, Jyoti shines. By worshipping Jyoti, a Hindu seeks God's blessings to acquire intelligence and wisdom (*jñāna*), attain love for all of God's creatures and secure divine guidance for spiritual progress, leading to spiritual perfection.

Since Jyoti is present in all beings as the light of consciousness, social service and reverence for all forms of life are the hallmarks of Jyoti worship. Jyoti shrines have been erected at many temples, including Houston Sri Meenakshi Temple, New York Maha Vallabh Ganapati Temple, and Los Angeles Sri Venkateswara Temple.

JYOTI

Color Plate 1

GANESHA

Color Plate 2

Color Plate 3

SHIVA

Color Plate 4

DURGÃ

Color Plate 5

LAKSHMÎ

Color Plate 6

Color Plate 7

SÎTÃ, RÃMA, LAKSHMANA AND HANÛMÃN

Color Plate 8

RĀDHĀ AND KRISHNA

Color Plate 9

Chapter 4
Hindu Scriptures—an Overview

Hindu religious literature, the most ancient writings in the world, is of two types: primary scriptures (*Sruti*) and secondary scriptures (*Smriti*). The Sruti scriptures are of divine origin, whose truths were directly revealed to ancient *rishis* (sages) in their deep meditations. The Smriti scriptures are of human origin and were written to explain the Sruti writings and make them understandable and meaningful to the general population. Sruti scriptures include the four Vedas (*Rig, Yajur, Sāma and Atharva*) and the *Bhagavad Gîtā*, and constitute the highest religious authority in Hindu religion. Smriti scriptures include five distinct groups of writings as shown in Table 2.

The Vedas are groups of hymns and chants containing religious and spiritual insights of the ancient sages and seers. Each Veda consists of four parts: *Mantras* (or *Samhitās*), *Brāhmanas, Āranyakas,* and *Upanishads.* Mantras are poetic compositions and hymns of supplication and incantation addressed to the deities, the symbolic representations of the Supreme Lord. The Brāhmanas deal with rules and regulations for proper performance of religious rites, rituals and ceremonies. The Āranyakas (as forest books) provide the symbolic and spiritual basis for the Brāhmanas. The Upanishads reveal the knowledge about Brahman and are known as *Vedānta,* meaning "end of the Vedas." They are the concluding portions of the Vedas.

Whereas the Upanishads represent the essence of the Vedas, the Bhagavad Gîtā, the most popular scripture of Hindus, contains the essence of the Upanishads. The Vedas reflect the dawn of spiritual insight, the Upanishads and the Bhagavad Gîtā contain the full splendor of a spiritual vision.

Message of Hindu Scriptures for Mankind

During their spiritual quest, the ancient rishis experienced sparks of divinity in all things and beings of the world. The vision of the Hindu scriptures is thus a vision of the unity of all existence, summarized as follows:

♦ There are many ways of conceiving the Supreme Reality (*Brahman*) and numerous ways of approaching It. To insist that one's own way is the only way is thus wrong and harmful.

♦ God is the source of goodness and truth. Man's goal in life is to seek union with Him. This union can be sought in many ways, all requiring sincerity of purpose, self-sacrifice and discipline.

♦ The highest religious experience is the one in which an individual transcends the intellect and realizes God immediately.

♦ The concept of "survival-of-the-fittest" is God's law for the animals. Harmlessness to all creatures is His law for humans.

♦ There is natural order (*rita*) inherent in the natural world. There must be moral order (*dharma*) inherent in human life. Everyone must be responsible for his (or her) actions and their consequences (*karma*). We cannot blame God for our ills.

♦ Individual responsibility and one's ethics are a foundation for individual happiness and social stability.

♦ The universe is a wheel of sacrifice (*yajña*). At the beginning the Supreme Lord performed self-sacrifice to create the universe and set the wheel in motion. The water sacrifices to form clouds, the clouds sacrifice to make rains, the rains sacrifice to grow food, and the food sacrifices to feed humans. In turn, humans must sacrifice for the welfare of the Mother Earth and all its creatures.

♦ There is no intrinsic evil in Nature nor any evil force in the world to oppose God. Man commits evil only due to ignorance (*māyā*).

♦ Love, freedom and peace are fruits of the tree of divine consciousness, which can be planted by worshipping God regularly and systematically through yoga, meditation, study of scriptures, by performing religious rites and ceremonies—as enjoined by scriptures—and selfless work.

HINDU SCRIPTURES SUMMARIZED

SRUTI (Primary Scriptures)	
Vedas (Rig, Sāma, Yajur & Atharva)	Include religion, philosophy, art, medicine, science, technology, language, music, etc.
Bhagavad Gîtā	A spiritual discourse between Lord Krishna and warrior Arjuna; summary of the Upanishads.
SMRITI (Secondary Scriptures)	
1. Dharma Shāstras	**Law Codes**
◆ Manu Smriti	Includes laws for individual happiness and social stability; social philosophy.
◆ Artha Shāstra	Includes guidelines for ruling the country.
◆ Kāma Shāstra	An ancient manual of love and pleasure.
2. Itihāsas	**Epics**
◆ Rāmāyana	Describes the life story of Lord Rāma; a most popular instrument of religious teaching.
◆ Mahābhārata	Includes the story of the Mahābhārata war. The Bhagavad Gîtā is a part of the Mahābhārata.
3. Purānas	**Mythology** There are 18 major Purānas: six devoted to worship of Shiva, six to Vishnu, and six to Brahma.
4. Āgamas & Tantras	**Sectarian Scriptures** Scriptures of the three major theological traditions: Shaivism, Vaishnavism, and Shaktism.
5. Darshanas	**Manuals of Philosophy**
◆ Brahma Sûtra	Vedānta philosophy of Sage Vyāsa
◆ Mîmāmsā Sûtra	Philosophy of rites and rituals of Sage Jaimini
◆ Nyāya Sûtra	Logical analysis of Sage Gautama (not Buddhā)
◆ Vaisheshika Sûtra	Atomic school of philosophy of Sage Kanāda
◆ Sānkhya Sûtras	Sānkhya philosophy of Sage Kapila
◆ Yoga Sûtras	Yoga philosophy of Sage Patānjali

Table 2

Chapter 5
Principal Hindu Doctrines

Although there are numerous doctrines in Hindu scriptures, the major doctrines of the Hindu religious tradition can be represented by the letters of the words *HINDU DHARMA* as explained below:

Harmony of Religions   **D**octrine of Karma
Ishvara (God)   **H**uman Life, the Goal of
Non-Violence (Ahimsã)   **Ã**tman, the Divinity of
Dharma   **R**eligious Discipline
Unity of Existence   **M**oksha (liberation)
                                  Avatãra, the Doctrine of

Harmony of Religions

Hindu sages declare that there is no one religion that teaches an exclusive road to salvation. All genuine spiritual paths are valid and all great religions are like the branches of a tree—the tree of religion. The Bhagavad Gîtã declares, "In whatever way they [human beings] love Me (God), in the same way they find My love. Various are the ways for them, but in the end they all come to Me." (BG 4.11)

Practical significance: This doctrine lays foundation for the Hindu ideal of universal harmony. The Hindu attitude of religious acceptance is Hindu Dharma's greatest gift to mankind.

Ishvara (God)

There is but one Supreme Being, Who is absolute existence, absolute knowledge, and absolute bliss (*sat-chid-ãnanda*). He is both immanent and transcendent, and both Creator and Unmanifest Reality. There is no duality of God and the world, but only unity. God can be worshipped and prayed in the form of a chosen deity (*Ishta Devatā*) in the temples and in home shrines.

Practical Significance: Being a God-loving religion and not a God-fearing one, Hindu Dharma relies upon self-knowledge through yoga and meditation rather than on dogma or blind faith.

Non-Violence (Ahimsā)

Ahimsā means non-violence (in thought, word and deed), non-injury, or non-killing. Hindu Dharma teaches that all forms of life are different manifestations of Brahman. We must therefore not be indifferent to the sufferings of any of God's creatures.

Practical Significance: This doctrine creates love for humans between themselves as well as with other forms of life, and encourages the protection of our environment. "That mode of living which is founded upon a total harmlessness towards all creatures or (in case of actual necessity) upon a minimum of such harm, is the highest morality." (Mahābhārata Shāntiparva 262.5-6)

The Doctrine of Dharma

The thought of *dharma* generates deep confidence in the Hindu mind in cosmic justice. This is reflected in the often-quoted maxims: "The righteous side will have the victory." "Truth only prevails, not falsehood." "Dharma kills if it is killed; dharma protects if it is protected." "The entire world rests on dharma."

Dharma is the law that maintains the cosmic order as well as the individual and social order. Dharma sustains human life in harmony with nature. When we follow dharma, we are in conformity with the law that sustains the universe. Dharma is of four kinds: universal dharma (*rita*), human dharma (*ashram dharma*), social dharma (*varana dharma*), and individual dharma *(svadharma)*. All four dharmas together are called *sanātana dharma*, the orginal name of Hindu religion (see page 7).

Universal dharma includes the natural laws associated with the physical phenomenon of the universe, such as the laws of matter, science, and planetary motions. Human dharma means the human actions which maintain the individual, social, and environmental order. Social dharma is exemplified in human actions associated with

professional, social, community and national duties and responsibilities. Individual dharma consists of individual actions associated
with one's individual duties and responsibilities.

The Hindu doctrine of dharma states that right action must be
performed for the sake of righteousness, and good must be done for
the sake of goodness, without any expectation of receiving something
in return. The question arises as to what is right? Hindu scriptures
include the following guidance that should be used to determine what
is right under given circumstances:

⇨ Individual actions (*svadharma*) which are based upon truth,
   ahimsā, and moral values are considered righteous actions.

⇨ Political, social, and community-related activities, which are
   based upon unselfishness, truth, ahimsā, and moral and ethical
   values are defined as right actions.

⇨ Actions that arise as a consequence of one's stage of life (*ashram dharma*) are considered good. The dharma of a student is
   to acquire knowledge and skills, whereas the dharma of a
   householder is to raise the family, and that of a retiree is to
   advise and guide the younger generations.

⇨ Actions that are associated with one's profession (*varna dharma*) are considered right actions. The duty of a soldier may be
   to take the life of an enemy, whereas the duty of a doctor is to
   save the life, including that of an enemy.

⇨ Actions which ensure adherence to the laws of the land are
   righteous actions. If the laws are unjust, they must be changed
   through democratic means and non-violence.

⇨ In the event of a conflict between individual and social dharma,
   the social dharma takes precedence. "He who understands his
   duty to society truly lives. All others shall be counted among
   the dead," declares Tirukural, a Hindu scripture.

⇨ "What you desire for yourself, you should desire for others.
   What you do not like others to do to you, you should not do to
   others." (Mahābhārata, Shāntiparva, 258)

Chapter 5

Practical Significance: Dharma provides a rational approach to distinguish right from wrong and good from evil. Duties and responsibilities are emphasized more than rights and privileges.

Unity of Existence

Science has revealed that what we call matter is essentially energy. Hindu sages have declared that the cosmic energy is a manifestation of the Universal Spirit (*Brahman*). The entire universe is a play between Brahman, or the cosmic consciousness, and the cosmic energy. Brahman has become all things and beings of the world. Thus we are all interconnected in subtle ways.

Practical Significance: This doctrine encourages universal brotherhood, reverence for all forms of life, and respect for our environment. There is no racial, cultural or religious superiority. There are differences on the surface, but deep down there is perfect unity, as All is in One and One is in all.

Doctrine of Karma—see Chapter 6

The Four Ends of Human Life

The four ends of human life are *dharma, artha, kāma,* and *moksha*. Dharma is the first human goal and forms the foundation for the pursuit of the other three goals. Dharmic actions are those individual, social, political, and professional actions which are based upon the four virtues—truth, ahimsā, morality and ethics. Artha means to earn wealth in accordance with dharma. Kāma is to satisfy one's mental and intellectual desires in accordance with dharma. Moksha denotes spiritual perfection, which is attained automatically when one leads a life that is dedicated to dharma.

Every child born on this earth is required to repay three debts in his (or her) lifetime. These three debts are akin to the three mortgages on one's life. The first debt is to God and the repayment requires regular prayers and worship, and selfless service to all of God's creatures.

The second debt is to the sages and saints, who have revealed truths in scriptures. The repayment of this debt arises from service to the needy, handicapped, sick and poor, and less fortunate. The third debt is to one's ancestors, parents and teachers. The repayment of this debt means raising one's family in accordance with the moral and ethical principles of dharma. To help an individual repay the above three debts, Hindu sages have organized life into four stages: studentship *(Brahmachārya Āshrama)*, householder stage *(Grhastha Āshrama)*, retirement *(Vānaprastha Āshrama)*, and renunciation *(Sannyāsa Āshrama)*.

During studentship one must acquire knowledge and skills necessary to perform duties and responsibilities in adult life, i.e. the householder stage. Retirement means a life of spirituality and gradual withdrawal from active life, to pass on skills to the next generation and begin devoting time to meditation and contemplation. Renunciation is the last stage of life in which one devotes full-time to meditation and contemplation on one's own self.

Practical Significance: The concept of the four ends and three debts generates awareness of one's duties and responsibilities, provides moral and ethical direction to life, encourages family values, and helps one to organize life for individual accomplishments. The Hindu concept of the four stages *(āshramas)* of life provides a road map for life's journey from the first stage of learning to the final stage where the Divinity alone is the focus and support.

The Divinity of Ātman (soul)

Each human being, regardless of religion, geographic region, color, or creed is in reality Ātman clothed in a physical body. An individual is not born a sinner, but becomes a victim of *māyā* (cosmic ignorance). Just as darkness quickly disappears upon the appearance of light, an individual's delusion vanishes when he gains self-knowledge.

Practical Significance: This doctrine eliminates fear of God, encourages divine love, promotes freedom of thought, and removes fear and guilt which are psychological barriers to human growth.

Religious Discipline

Hindus believe that wisdom is not an exclusive possession of any particular race or religion. Since a laborer requires a different kind of religion than a scholar, Hindu Dharma allows an individual to select a religious discipline in accordance with one's own religious yearning and spiritual competence. Hindu Dharma recommends the guidance of a spiritually awakened master (*guru*) for attaining perfection in life. If a devotee on the spiritual path is likened to a traveler, then the guru is the traveler's guide who provides the road map and other helpful information needed to reach the destination successfully.

Practical Significance: This doctrine minimizes religious manipulation and control and provides everyone with absolute freedom of thought in religious matters. One is free to question any belief and practice until one is convinced of the truth behind it.

Moksha

The ultimate goal of Hindu religious life is to attain spiritual freedom (*moksha*, i.e. freedom from the cycle of birth and death in the phenomenal world), or union with God. Moksha is the birth right of every individual and is automatically attained when one leads a life dedicated to *dharma*, *artha*, and *kāma*. Moksha is akin to the top of a three-step ladder, and after taking the three steps of dharma, artha, and kāma, one will automatically reach the top.

Practical Significance: This doctrine encourages individual effort and understanding for attaining perfection in life. Each soul evolves toward union with God by his own effort. No savior can achieve this for him. There is no supernatural power that randomly determines our destinies. We are the makers of our own destinies. Self-effort and Divine grace together lead to spiritual perfection.

The Doctrine of Avatāra (Incarnation)

Hindus believe that God incarnates Himself on earth (*avatāra*) to uphold righteousness, whenever there is a loss of virtue. The Bhagavad Gîtā thus declares, "Whenever there is a decline of righteousness and predominance of unrighteousness, I (God) embody Myself. For the protection of the good and for the destruction of the evil-doers and for the re-establishment of righteousness, I am born from age to age." (Bhagavad Gîtā 4.6-4.7)

Practical Significance: This doctrine encourages righteousness and fosters hope for mankind, since divine intervention eventually destroys evil and restores balance in the world.

Chapter 6
Law of Karma

The word *karma* literally means 'deed or action,' but implies the entire cycle of cause and its effects. According to the Law of Karma, every human action—in thought, word, or deed—inevitably leads to results, good or bad, depending upon the moral quality of the action. There is no such thing as action without results. "As we sow, so shall we reap," is the unerring law which governs all deeds. The Law of Karma conserves the moral consequences of all actions, and conditions our future lives accordingly. We ourselves create our future destinies by our own choices each minute. Every child born in this world is born to work out its own past deeds.

The doctrine of karma is the answer provided by Hindus to the questions of why suffering and inequalities exist in the world: "Why should one person be different from another in his looks, abilities, and character? Why is one born a king and another a beggar? A just and merciful God cannot create such inequalities." The doctrine of karma, a law of actions and their retribution, can be viewed as the law of causation (cause and effect) applied to the moral realm. The law that every action has a reaction works in the scientific world as well as in the moral world.

The doctrine of karma is based upon the principle of cause and effect. This doctrine of cause and effect differs from the Christian notion that God punishes the wicked and rewards the virtuous. The underlying basis for this difference is that Hindu religion is a god-loving religion rather than a god-fearing one.

Karma is neither predestination nor fatalism. Fatalism and predestination imply that individuals are bound by circumstances or by some outside power and, as such, cannot free themselves with their own effort. That is exactly opposite of karma. The Law of Karma is actually the law of harmony and equilibrium. It adjusts wisely, intelligently and equitably each effect to its cause. But, it is also the law of opportunity, which allows an individual to change his past for a better future. If we understand karma as the law of order and opportunity, we will become self-reliant and understand that we cannot and should not escape responsibility.

Operation of the Law of Karma

The past karma of an individual consists of two parts, *prārabdha karma* and *sañchita karma* (see Figure 2). Prārabdha karma is the part of one's past karma which is to bear fruit in the present life of the individual. Sañchita karma is accumulated karma of the previous births which is to bear fruit in the future. Prārabdha karma of an individual consists of two components: fixed and variable. The fixed component of karma is beyond our control and consists of that component of the past karma which determines one's parents, the family and the country in which a child must be born, the general features of the physical body that the child will eventually develop, and the social and religious environment in which the child must grow.

The variable component of the past karma remains latent in the subconscious mind of the child in the form of samskāras (natural habits and tendencies). It is this variable part of the past karma that one can overcome by initiative and free will. The level of success one can achieve in diluting the effects of the variable component, however, depends upon the power of the samskāras and the strength of the individual will.

The past karma of an ordinary human being is either good, bad, or mixed. An individual's particular incarnation is determined by the overall balance of past karma. If the overall balance is positive (i.e. overall good karma), the individual will be born in an environment that would be naturally conducive toward the onward progress of his soul. In a particular incarnation, only those innate tendencies (samskāras) are manifested for which conditions are favorable in that incarnation. The right environment is essential for manifestation of the samskāras. For example, if an individual is born as a professor (because of his overall good karma) and if he had been a gambler in his past incarnations, his innate gambling tendency will not find the right environment to manifest itself in the academic environment of his vocation. However, if he happens to be in the company of gamblers at a weekend party, he will exhibit a natural love for gambling because of the residual impressions of his past karma.

Every human action, be it physical or mental, produces two effects. First, depending upon the moral quality of an action, the appropriate fruits of the action will be rewarded later, either in the same life or in a future life. Secondly, the action leaves residual impressions (samskāras) on the subconscious mind of the individual. These samskāras generate thought waves (vrittis) and thereby determine the character of the individual. Thus, actions determine the personal conduct and this conduct molds the character, in a revolving chain of cause and effect. The Brihadāranyaka Upanishad declares thus: "A man becomes good by performing good deeds and evil by performing evil deeds."

Free Will

In the Hindu view, ātman (soul, self or sprit) is the source of the human will. Since ātman is divine and immortal, the human will is potentially powerful. However, due to the presence of the cosmic ignorance (māyā or avidyā), human will is generally weak and the individual lacks firm conviction and God-consciousness. Human will can be sharpened and strengthened by yoga, meditation, prayers, positive thinking, right environment, and association (satsangh) with the pure-minded persons. According to the philosophy of yoga, the negative thought waves which arise in the human mind due to samskāras of the past karma, can be neutralized by introducing positive thought waves generated by human will.

When an apple falls from a tree, the fall of the apple itself is caused by the law of gravitation. However, the consequences of this event are not only determined by the law of gravitation, but also by

OPERATION OF THE LAW OF KARMA

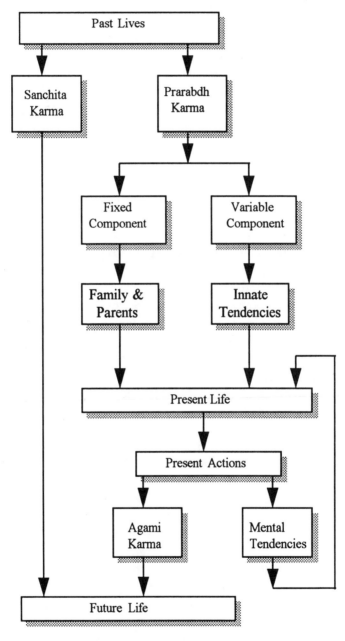

FIGURE 2

the law of conservation of energy. Just the same way, the consequences of human actions are determined by the doctrine of karma as
well as the doctrine of free will. The negative samskāras of the past
karma can be overcome by human will. In Hindu view, what separa-
tes a saint and a sinner is only time. With right knowledge and effort,
a sinner of today can be a saint of tomorrow. As Dr. Rādhākrishnan
says, "The cards of life are given to us [in the form of samskāras], but
we can play them as we wish, and win or lose, as we play."

The Role of Parents and Teachers

When one commits a murder, two possibilities exist. Either the
person is creating a brand new karma (*agami karma*) by misusing his
free will, or his action is motivated by the negative samskāras of his
past actions. In either case he is totally responsible for his actions.
He could have been helped if his free will had been strengthened by
yoga, meditation, prayers, positive thinking, and right environment.
This responsibility squarely falls on the society in general, and parents
and teachers in particular. The best time (and perhaps the only time!)
to implant good samskāras in a person is when the person is still
young and his negative samskāras are not yet ready to bear their bitter
fruit. The children in modern societies are constantly subjected to
negative samskāras of violence perpetuated by radio and television,
family conflicts, and lack of appropriate training of parents to
properly raise their children.

Unfortunately, in modern societies more attention is given to
development of the body than the mind. The educational institutions
generally teach skills that enable one to make a descent living to
maintain one's physical body, but no skills are generally taught to
nourish one's mind. Just as soap and shampoo clean the physical
body, yoga and meditation clean the mind by removing mental
impurities, such as fear, anger, lust, greed, jealousy, and conceit.
Yoga and meditation also strengthen the mind by increasing its
willpower. A strong mind is a virtuous mind and without virtue there
can be no happiness in this world. "One may gain political and social
independence, but if he is a slave to his passions and desires, he
cannot feel the pure joy of freedom," says Swāmī Vivekānanda.[30]

Chapter 6

Chapter 7
Popular Systems of Hindu Religious Thought

Hindu religious thought embodies a great variety of ideas, principles and practices, giving rise to various religious schools (*sampradāyas*). Each school venerates the Supreme Deity, which represents a particular aspect of the Ultimate Reality (*Brahman*). Each school has temples, *guru* lineages, religious leaders, pilgrimage centers, monastic communities, and sacred literature. Some of these schools hold such divergent views that each appears to be a complete religion in itself. Yet, they all believe in the central doctrines of Hindu religion, such as karma, dharma, reincarnation, divinity of the ātman, sacraments, deity worship, *guru-shishya* (teacher-disciple) tradition and the scriptural authority of the Vedas. None of these schools is in any way superior or inferior to the others. They simply represent different ways of approach to the same goal and are meant for various classes of people having different tastes, aptitudes, temperaments, and exhibiting various levels of spiritual development.

The Hindu religious systems have been classified by Adi Shankar-āchārya into six major paths, called *Shad-maths*. These are *Shaivism*, *Vaishnavism*, *Shāktism*, *Gānapathyam*, *Kaumāram*, and *Sauram* or *Jyotiam*.

Shaivism
The followers of Shaivism venerate the Ultimate Reality as Lord Shiva. This tradition has been traced back by scholars approximately 8000 years to the Indus Valley Civilization. The archeologists have discovered the so-called proto-*Pashupati* seals of this civilization, which depict Shiva as Lord *Pashupati*, seated in a yogic pose. There

are many schools of Shaivism, of which the six major systems are *Shaiva Siddhānta, Pāshupata Shaivism,* Kashmîr *Shaivism, Vîra Shaivism, Siddha Siddhānta,* and *Shiva Advaita.* These systems differ somewhat in their doctrines pertaining to the relationship between Shiva, the ātman and the world.

Most Hindus worship Lord Shiva as a member of the Hindu Trinity (see Chapter 3). However, the followers of Shaivism, called *Shaivas* or *Shaivites,* worship Him as the Ultimate Reality. The predominant philosophy of Shaivism is monistic-theism. According to this doctrine, Lord Shiva is both personal and impersonal. In the personal aspect, Shiva creates, controls, and pervades all that exists. In this aspect, Shiva is what other religions call God. Shaivism declares that there is nothing outside Shiva and, thus, recognizes the oneness of *Pati-pau-pāśa* (God-ātman-world). In the impersonal aspect, Shiva transcends all existence and in the liberated state the ātman is one with Shiva.

The main objects of Shiva worship are *shivalinga* and images of Shiva. Shivalinga means "Shiva symbol." The word *linga* is derived from the two Sanskrit words *laya* (dissolution) and *agaman* (recreation). Thus, *shivalinga* symbolizes that entity in which the creation merges at the time of dissolution and out of which the universe reappears at the beginning of the new cycle of creation.

Shivalinga consists of three parts. The bottom part which is four-sided remains under ground, the middle part which is eight-sided remains on a pedestal and the top part which is actually worshipped is round. The height of the round part is one-third of its circumference. The three parts symbolize Brahma at the bottom, Vishnu in the middle and Shiva on the top. The pedestal is provided with a passage for draining away the water that is poured on top by devotees.

The linga symbolizes both the creative and destructive power of the Lord and great sanctity is attached to it by the devotees. The *bānaliñgas* are very sacred objects of worship to the followers of Shaivism. These are the elliptical stones of a special kind found in the bed of the river Narmadā, one of the seven sacred rivers in India. Fresh flowers, pure water, young sprouts of *Kusha* (a holy grass) and *dûrvā* (called bent or panic grass), fruit, *bilva* leaves and sun-dried

Religious Tradition	Ishta Devatā (Personal God)	Auspicious Materials of Worship	Major Scriptures	Auspicious Mantra (see Note)
Shaivism	Shiva	red China roses, bilva leaves & durva (special grass)	Vedas, Shaiva Āgamas and Shaiva Purānas	Om Namah Shivāya
Vaishnavism	Vishnu	white flowers and tulasi leaves	Vedas, Vaishnava Āgamas and Purānas, Rāmāyana, Mahābhārata, and Bhagavad Gitā.	Om Namo Nārāyanāya; Om Namo Bhagavate Vasudevāya
Shāktism	Shakti	lotuses for Lakshmi, yellow flowers for Saraswati & red flowers for Durgā	Vedas, Shākta Āgamas and Purānas	Om Hrim Chandikāyai Namah
Gānapathyam	Ganesha	red flowers and durva (special grass)	Vedas and Skānda Purāna.	Om Sri Ganayshāya Namah; Om Gām Gam Ganapataye Namah
Kaumāram	Kārttikeya or Subramanya	flowers of all colors	Vedas and Purānas	Om Kārttikeya Namah
Sauram	Sun-god	red lotuses	Vedas and Purānas	Gāyatrī Mantra (see page 71)

Note: Each of these mantras is imbibed with mystic power and can be used in meditation for spiritual growth.

Table 3 — Popular Hindu Religious Traditions

rice are used in the ritual part of the Shiva worship. According to tradition, offering leaves of the *bilva* tree (wood-apple) is considered very auspicious for the worship of Lord Shiva.

Mahāshivarātri (the great night of Shiva) is an annual festival that falls on the fourteenth day of the dark fortnight of *Phālguna* (February-March), and is dedicated to the worship of Lord Shiva. On this day devotees sing *bhajans* (devotional songs) in honor of Shiva, recite Sanskrit *shlokas* (verses) from scriptures, offer prayers in the morning and evening, and some observe a fast throughout the day. People visit nearby temples of Shiva and offer prayers in large crowds. The prayers and worship continue late into the night when the devotees offer flowers, coconut, *bilva* leaves, fruits, and specially prepared sacred food to Shiva and His divine consort Pārvatī.

In mythology, Shiva is the husband of Pārvatī, the daughter of the Himalayas. They have two sons, Ganesha and Kārttikeya and daughter Jyoti. Their residence is the snow-clad mountain Kailāsh. The mythology depicts Shiva both as God of terror as well as benevolence. His five powers are revealment (offering grace to the devotees), concealment (obscuring by His power of māyā), creation, preservation, and dissolution. The major scriptures of Shaivism are Vedas, Shaiva Āgamas and Shaiva Purānas.

Vaishnavism

Vaishnavism venerates the Ultimate Reality as Lord Vishnu. This tradition began during the Vedic period when its earliest schools *Pañcharātra* and *Bhāgavata* became popular around 300 BCE. Modern day Vaishnavism includes five popular schools founded by Rāmānuja, Mādhva, Nimbārka, Vallabha and Chaitanya. These schools slightly differ in their doctrines pertaining to the relationship between Vishnu, the ātman and the world.

Most Hindus worship Lord Vishnu as a member of the Hindu Trinity. However, the followers of Vaishnavism, called *Vaishnavas* or *Vaishnavites*, worship Lord Vishnu as the Ultimate Reality. Although the philosophy of Vaishnavism includes dualism of Madhva, qualified dualism of Rāmānuja, and nearly monistic views of Vallabha, the predominant philosophy of Vaishnavism is dualism. According to this doctrine, there are two categories of the Ultimate Reality. Lord Vishnu as personal God is the Absolute Reality, and the ātmans (individuals souls) are the relative realities, eternally distinct from each other and Lord Vishnu, but dependent on Him.

The doctrine of incarnation (*avatāra*) is fundamental to all Hindus, especially to Vaishnavas. This doctrine is declared in the Bhagavad Gîtā when Krishna tells Arjuna, "Whenever unrighteousness increases and evil becomes triumphant, I incarnate on earth in age after age for protection of the good, for the destruction of the evildoers, and for the re-establishment of virtue and righteousness." (BG 4.7,4.8) Each avatāra is assumed by Vishnu for a particular end and as the situation demands. The number of avatāras of Vishnu are generally accepted to be ten, with Rāma and Krishna being the two most popular among Hindus.

Vaishnavism stresses complete surrender (*prapatti*) to Lord Vishnu and His incarnations and advocates devotion (*bhakti*) as the highest spiritual discipline. The objects of worship are the images of Vishnu and His incarnations, and *sālagrāmas*, small stones of different colors (predominantly black) recovered from the bed of the river Gandakî, one of the tributaries of the Ganges river in India. Sālagrāmas are river-worn, fossilized ammonite shells with one or more holes in the side, having several spiral grooves resembling the wheel emblem of Vishnu.

Fresh flowers, water, fruit, leaves of the *tulasî* plant are used in the ritual part of the worship of Lord Vishnu and His incarnations. According to tradition, offering leaves of the *tulasî* plant to the deities of Vishnu is considered very auspicious in the worship of Lord Vishnu. One of the unique features of the Vaishnava worship is kîrtana, which consists of choral singing of the names and deeds of Lord Vishnu and His incarnations, accompanied by drums and cymbals and synchronized with rhythmic bodily movements. The major scriptures of Vaishnavism are Vedas, Āgamas, Purānas, Rāmāyana, Mahābhārata, and Bhagavad Gîtā.

Shāktism

Shakti means "creative energy," and *Shāktism* means "Doctrine of the Creative Energy." Shāktism venerates the Ultimate Reality as the Divine Mother—*Shakti* or *Devi*—of the universe. Archeologists have recovered thousands of female statuettes at the Mehrgarh village in India, which indicate that Shakti worship existed in India as far back as 5500 BCE. There are references to the female deities in the Rig Veda, including a popular Hymn to the Divine Mother (Devî-sûkta, X.125), which holds special sanctity to Hindus in general and *Shāktas* (the followers of Shāktism) in particular.

Shāktism visualizes the Ultimate Reality as having two aspects, transcendent and immanent. Shiva is the transcendent aspect, the supreme cosmic consciousness, and Shakti is the supreme creative energy. Shiva and Shakti are God and God's creative energy inseparably connected. Metaphorically, Shiva and Shakti are an inseparable divine couple, representing the male and female principle in creation.

Shāktism greatly resembles Shaivism, but Shiva is considered solely transcendent and is not worshipped. Like Shaivism, the goal of Shāktism is to unite with Shiva. Such unity is possible only with the grace of the Divine Mother, Who unfolds as *icchā shakti* (the power of desire, will and love), *kriyā shakti* (the power of action), and *jñanā shakti* (the power of knowledge and wisdom). According to the Tantra philosophy, the spiritual center at the crown of the head (*sahasrāra chakra*) is the abode of Shiva. Likewise, the spiritual center at the base of the spine (*mûlādhāra*) is the abode of shakti. Normally shakti is latent in the *mûlādhāra*. Through a spiritual discipline, shakti is awakened and it rises through the spine and unites with Shiva in the *sahasrāra*. When this energy transformation occurs, the individual attains cosmic consciousness and is said to have realized the Self.

Within Shāktism, Shiva is the unmanifest Absolute and Shakti is the Divine Mother of the manifest creation. The Divine Mother is worshipped in both the fierce and benign forms. The fierce forms of Goddess include Kālî, Durgā, Chandî, Chamundî, Bhadrakālî and Bhairavî. The benign forms of Goddess include Umā, Gaurî, Ambikā,

Pārvatî, Maheshvarî, Lalitā, Lakshmî, Saraswatî and Annapûrnā. The major scriptures of Shāktism are *Vedas, Shākta Āgamas* and *Purānas*.

Gānapathyam

Ganesha, the elephant-headed deity (see Chapter 3), represents that aspect of the Ultimate Reality which removes obstacles. Hindus, therefore, invoke Lord Ganesha at the beginning of all undertakings, whether religious, spiritual or worldly, for Lord Ganesha removes obstacles and brings success to the enterprise. Ganesha is also called *Vighneshvara*, meaning "the Lord presiding over the obstacles." In the Rig Veda (2.23.1), Ganesha is the name of *Brihapati*, the Lord of prayer (the Holy Word). In mythology, Ganesha is the first son of the divine couple Shiva and Pārvatî.

Most Hindus worship Ganesha along with other deities, but *Gānapatyas*, followers of Gānapathyam, venerate Lord Ganesha exclusively as the form of the Ultimate Reality (*Brahman*) that is accessible to the mind, senses and (through devotional practices) the heart.

Gānapatyas regard Morayā Gosāvî (1651 AD), the famous devotee of Ganesha, as their spiritual progenitor. Tradition holds that Morayā experienced a series of visions of Ganesha at a shrine at Moragaon, near Poona, India.

An annual ten-day festival, *Ganesha Chaturthi*, is held in August-September to celebrate the birth of Ganesha. During this time elaborate *pujās* are held in homes and temples. At the end of the festival clay images *(murtis)* of Ganesha are taken in a spectacular procession, called *Visarjana*, to the seashore, river or lake, where they are immersed in water to symbolize the merging of Ganesha with the ocean of consciousness. In November-December, devotees observe a 21-day festival. During this period daily pūjās are offered, fasting on water is observed throughout the day, and a full meal is taken after sunset. The major scriptures of this tradition are Vedas, Ganesha Purāna, and Mudgala Purāna.

Chapter 7

Kaumāram

The followers of this tradition venerate Lord Kārttikeya, also called by other names such as Murugan, Kumāra, Skanda, Subramanya, and Shanmukhanātha, as their *Ishta Devatā* (personal-God). Lord Kārttikeya represents the power of the Ultimate Reality (Brahman) that destroys ignorance, bestows divine knowledge, upholds dharma (righteousness), removes worries, and strengthens human will.

In mythology, Kārttikeya and Ganesha are the two sons of Shiva and Pārvatî. In popular pictures and images, Kārttikeya is shown holding a spear which symbolizes His divine power to destroy ignorance and unrighteousness (see Chapter 3).

Lord Kārttikeya is worshipped in homes and temples throughout the year. On the day of Vaikāsi Vishākham in May-June, elaborate pujās and special ceremonies (*abhishekam*) are conducted in homes and temples. His protection and grace are specially invoked on the day of *Skanda Shashthî*, which falls on the sixth day after the new moon in October-November. In January-February, another holy festival (*Tai Pusam*) is observed in honor of Lord Kārttikeya. On this occasion the devotees fast and perform public penance to invoke the Lord's blessings to remove sins, pride and vanity, and bestow spiritual knowledge. Special pujās are performed in honor of Lord Kārttikeya every month on *Krittikā nakshatra* and *Shashthi*, the sixth day after the new moon.

Sauram

The power of the sun to dispel darkness, illuminate the world, and nourish mankind is recognized by Hindus as an aspect of the infinite power of the Ultimate Reality (Brahman). The worship of this triple power of the Divine, symbolized by the Vedic deity Sûrya, the Sun-god, is called Sauram. Sûrya is worshipped by Hindus as an object of meditation during many physical exercises. Sacred verses selected from the epic and Pûranic literature are daily recited by devout Hindus early in the morning before commencing the day's work. The best known of the hymns to the sun is one from Rāmāyana, that was imparted to Rāma during his battle with Rāvana.

Hindus in general worship the sun every year on the seventh day after the new moon in the month which corresponds to January-February. Sacred mantras are recited for the special worship of the sun, especially on Sundays, birthdays, and at other special functions. Prostrations are made to the sun after each tenth mantra until one hundred and thirty-two prostrations have been completed. These prostrations are done in the form of a physical exercise, called *Sûrya-Namaskâra*, which consists of adorations to the sun in the form of a set of twelve simple poses in Hatha Yoga.[29]

The following most sacred Rigvedic prayer, named after its meter, is called *Gâyatrî*, meaning "the savior of the singer." It is considered to be the mantra of all mantras, the most potent mantra, repeated as many times as possible by Hindus daily in *pûjâ* and personal chanting to venerate the sun as the Creator (*Savitar*). The mystic power of this mantra is so high that it is called *Vedâmatri*, meaning "Mother of the Vedas." *Gâyatrî Mantra* is imparted to a young boy for initiation into Vedic tradition.

> "*Om bhûr bhuvah svah, tatsavitur varenyam, bhargo devasya, dhîmahi, dhiyo yo nah prachodayât, Om.*" (Rig Veda 3.62.10)

> "God is the giver of life, the dispeller of miseries, and bestower of happiness. We meditate upon that adorable effulgence of the resplendent vivifier, Savitar. May He stimulate our intellects."

Gâyatrî Mantra is a universal prayer, open to the people of all time and clime, without any limitation of color, creed, race or religious affiliation. "This prayer requires us, not to lose ourselves, but to find our true Self, naked and without the mask of falsehood, to live our lives on the highest plane of self-criticism and human aspiration," says Sarvepâlli Râdhâkrishnan.[5]

Chapter 7

Chapter 8
Moral and Ethical Ideals of Hindus

Ethics can be described as the science of morality, and morality as the living of a virtuous life. Hindus place greater emphasis on the attitude of the mind rather than on postulation of the elaborate theories of what is right and what is wrong. Accordingly, the Hindu vision of morality and ethics is characterized by the following considerations:

♦ Morality proceeds from the inner spirit of man. In Hindu view, one's motive is as important in the performance of an action as the action itself. When the heart is pure and free from lust and greed, whatever one does to perform one's duties has a high moral value.

♦ Harmlessness to all creatures is the highest morality.

♦ There are four sources of right conduct: Vedas, the *Smriti* (secondary scriptures), the conduct of wise persons, and the individual's own judgment. [8]

♦ In times of confusion and crisis regarding what is right and what is wrong, one's own conscience is the sole guide. "In times of doubt, O, son of Kunti [Arjuna], one must decide using one's own good sense." [9]

♦ An individual is ultimately responsible for his own actions, i.e. the Law of Karma. He is also responsible for the actions of others if he induces or forces them to perform such actions.

♦ Hindus declare that loyalty to one's moral values is the highest loyalty, and of all the losses, loss of one's character and loss of judgment are the worse. [7]

Yamas and Niyamas[16] - Moral and Ethical Ideals of Hindus	
1. *Ahimsā* (non-injury)	Don't harm others by word, deed or thought.
2. *Satya* (truthfulness)	Refrain from lying and betraying promises.
3. *Asteya* (nonstealing)	Don't steal, covet or enter into debt.
4. *Brahmachārya* (controlling sex)	Observe celibacy when single, and faithfulness in marriage.
5. *Kshamā* (forgiveness)	Restrain from intolerance and ill will.
6. *Dhriti* (firmness)	Overcome fear, indecision, and fickleness.
7. *Dayā* (compassion)	Conquer callous and insensitive feelings.
8. *Ārjava* (honesty)	Renounce fraud, cheating and stealing.
9. *Mitāhāra*	Refrain from overeating and consuming meat.
10. *Shaucha* (purity)	Observe purity of the body, mind and intellect.
11. *Hrî* (remorse)	Be modest and show remorse for misconduct.
12. *Santosha* (contentment)	Don't be a slave to the senses. Seek joy and serenity in the Self.
13. *Dāna* (tithing)	Give generously without thought of reward. The more you give, the more you get.
14. *Āstikya* (faith)	Have unwavering faith in God's grace.
15. *Pûjana* (worship)	Perform daily worship and meditation.
16. *Shravana* (hearing of scriptures)	Study scriptures, listen to the teachings of the wise, and faithfully follow *guru's* advice.
17. *Mati* (cognition)	Sharpen the intellect with *guru's* guidance.
18. *Vrata* (sacred vows)	Observe scriptural injunctions faithfully.
19. *Japa* (chanting)	Chant God's names and sacred *mantras* daily.
20. *Tapas* (austerity)	Perform *sādhana* (spiritual discipline) as outlined by the *guru*.

Table 4

Chapter 9
Hindu View of a Harmonious Family

Every human being is potentially divine and the goal of life is to express this divinity by performing useful work. A harmonious family is an institution which provides the energy and inspiration to bring forth one's divinity. A child of a harmonious family becomes a divine personality.

Expressing one's inherent divinity is akin to entering a house that has four doors, with each door having a unique key. Each door must be opened to gain entry into the house. There is one road that leads to this house. In this example, the four doors are *dedication*, *contribution*, *learning* and *responsibility*. The four keys are *love*, *recognition*, *sharing* and *trust*. The name of the road is *offer* and *receive* (*sammarpan* and *swêkãr*). The following illustrates which key opens which door:

Offer			*& Receive*		
	⇨	Love		⇨	Dedication
	⇨	Recognition		⇨	Contribution
	⇨	Sharing		⇨	Learning
	⇨	Trust		⇨	Responsibility

Love and Dedication

Love is accepting a person as he (or she) is and helping him to grow. Love is a divine feeling which is beyond likes and dislikes. Dedication is self-sacrificing devotion to whatever one does. Dedication builds attitudes in people. Positive attitudes are necessary to perform useful work in the world.

74

Love and dedication are two aspects of the same relationship. When parents are loving, the children are dedicated. When the children are dedicated, the parents are loving. When the teacher is loving, the students are dedicated and when the students are dedicated, the teacher is loving. The love-dedication relationship brings out noble qualities of the child and helps him to grow and establish harmonious relationships within the family and with the outside world.

Recognition and Contribution

While attitudes are necessary, abilities and skills are required for an active and contributing personality. Abilities and skills are developed by performing useful work. It is essential to ensure an atmosphere of daily useful work in the family. When children contribute to useful work, they can perform useful work for the society, nation and humanity in their adult lives.

Recognition and contribution are two sides of the same interaction. Recognition begets contribution and the contribution begets recognition. Parents are the starting point. When parents recognize and appreciate, children will contribute more and more. When children contribute, parents will appreciate more and more.

Sharing and Learning

Dedication and contribution alone are not sufficient. Knowledge is necessary to perform useful work in the world. Knowledge comes from learning, and learning comes from sharing. While there is an end for every teaching, there is no end for learning. When parents continuously share their knowledge and experience with their children, the children continuously learn.

Sharing and learning are two aspects of the same relationship. When parents share, children learn and when children learn, parents share. Sharing is the best way of teaching. Sharing encourages learning. With a positive attitude towards work and learning, children can grow into noble personalities.

Trust and Responsibility

Positive attitude, dedication and knowledge alone are not sufficient for a person to express divinity. Responsibility is another key factor. A responsible person is an enriched person. Assuming responsibility for the family, society, nation, and humanity is divinity.

It is essential to inculcate a sense of responsibility into children, a task for the parents. The parents cannot perform this task unless they are responsible themselves. Trust and responsibility are two aspects of the same interaction. When parents trust their children, the children take on responsibility, and in turn develop increasing trust with their parents. A trusted person is a divine person.

Conclusions

⇨ A harmonious family is an institution which provides the energy and inspiration necessary to bring forth one's divinity.

⇨ The key to a harmonious family is the *offer and receive* philosophy (*sammarpan* and *swêkãr),* as taught by *rishis.* Family members must learn to rise above the *take and take* (a thief's philosophy), *take and give* (government philosophy), *give and take* (business philosophy) and adopt the *offer and receive* philosophy within the family.

⇨ The love-dedication relationship builds positive attitudes in children. As parents offer love and receive dedication, children will offer dedication and receive love.

⇨ Encourage children to participate in all aspects of daily work of the family. With positive attitudes and useful work, they will develop into noble and productive personalities in their adult lives.

⇨ Share knowledge with children. With positive attitudes, useful work and learning, they will become dedicated, knowledgeable and contributing personalities.

⇨ When parents trust children, children will take on responsibilities. A responsible person is an enriched person.

⇨ The three basic ideals of Hindu Dharma—*seva* (unselfish service), *vishva kutumbam* (universal family), and *sahaviryam* (togetherness in the family)—can be realized when children grow into responsible, knowledgeable, and dedicated contributors.

Chapter 9

Chapter 10
Hindu Reverence for Elders

A unique and magnificent feature of Hindu religious thought is that salvation is the birth right of each and every human being, and is attainable in due course of time (i.e. either in this life or in some future life) through spiritual practice and training. In the words of Betty Heimann, late professor of Sanskrit and Indian philosophy at Ceylon University, "It is an undeniable fact that no philosophy outside India makes such a varied and manifold use of [spiritual] instruction in order to visualize the supreme Truth. It is the very metaphysical bent of Hindu thought which makes room for this practical educational training." [13]

In Hindu culture, the elders (senior citizens) are considered to be the progenitors of spiritual instruction and training. The relationship with elders is, thus, viewed as a spiritual relationship by the young generation, and is revered as such. This reverence for old age in Hindu culture is reflected in the following Hindu etiquette and mannerism towards all elders in and outside one's family:

♦ Elders are received by standing up. One must stand up, if seated, in order to receive an elderly person.

♦ Elders are not called by their first or last names. They are addressed with conventional titles of courtesy such as Dr., Mr., Mrs., Ms., or personal titles such as Grandpa, Grandma, Uncle, Papa, and Mama. Depending upon one's level of familiarity with an elder(s), the word "Ji" is commonly added to the elder's first or last name (if male) or to the first name (if female) to form an appropriate address.

- In the presence of elders one sits or stands upright. Sitting with legs dangling, feet stretched or pointed towards or in the direction of elders, hands behind one's back or clapped around the neck, or arms folded are viewed as disrespectful to elders.

- In the presence of elders, smoking, chewing gum, drinking liquor, exhibiting overt behavior of love, affection, anger or bad temper are considered rude.

- Abusive, sarcastic, vulgar, or "street" language, boastful (words of self-praise), possessive (I, me, my or mine), or impersonal words are not used in communication with elders.

- When talking to an elder, one should always look towards the elder person. Looking towards other directions or rotating one's head or eyes while talking to an elder are considered rude and disrespectful.

- When elders are talking or discussing, a junior person addresses questions or converses with only the eldest person in the group. Addressing questions or conversing with junior persons in such a group, unless specifically permitted by the eldest person, is deemed as rude.

- When walking with an elder, one either walks in step with the elder or within a step behind the elder. Walking ahead of elders is deemed discourteous and disrespectful.

- In home or at the dinner table the elders are seated first before others take their seats. At public places (such as a bus or train) elders are offered seats first before others occupy their seats. When getting into a car, a person opens the door for elders and lets them sit first before others take their seats.

- Elders are not confronted in the presence of others. Any disagreements or differing viewpoints are discussed with them separately and only on a one-to-one basis.

Chapter 11
Daily Routine of a Devout Hindu

In addition to the normal activities associated with one's profession (*varna dharma*) and stage in life (*āshrama dharma*), the daily routine of a devout Hindu is to perform *pañcha mahā yagñas* (five daily duties) and *pañcha nitya karmas* (five constant duties). These are the minimal practices which guide a person in everyday life and ensure peace, material and spiritual prosperity.

Pañcha Mahā Yagñas (Five Daily Duties)

1. Worship God (*Deva Yagña*) in the form of a family deity (*Ishta Devatā*) in the home shrine through prayers and meditations. This practice helps one to become God-conscious in all daily activities. Additionally, this practice arouses a sense of togetherness in the family, since the family members worship together and participate in the rituals, chants, singing, and study of scriptures. Tradition says that "a family that prays together stays together."

2. Study Vedas and other scriptures (*Brahma Yagña*). This practice refreshes one's mind with sacred knowledge and also helps to preserve and enrich such knowledge.

3. Contemplate on the teachings of the sages, saints, holy men and women, and one's forefathers (*Pitri Yagña*). This practice is intended to serve as a reminder to preserve, enrich and continue one's cultural heritage and family values.

4. Provide food for those who are in need (*Bhuta Yagña*). This practice is intended to create the spirit of sharing with others.

5. Serve guests with love, respect, and reverence (*Nara Yagña*).
   This practice is the basis for the traditional hospitality of Hindu
   households.

Pañcha Nitya Karmas (Five Constant Duties)

1. *Dharma* (Righteousness): Live a virtuous life in accordance with
   the teachings of the scriptures. Cultivate virtues of purity, self-
   control, detachment, thinking of others first, truth and ahimsã. Be
   respectful of parents, teachers, and elders.

   Dharma also means performing all duties associated with
   one's normal profession, and individual and social obligations.
   Work must be performed purely for its own sake. This means
   that all actions must be performed for excellence and not merely
   for reward (*nishkama karma*). "Fix thy heart upon thy work, but
   not on its reward. Work not for a reward; but never cease to do
   thy work." (Bhagavad Gîtã 2.47)

2. *Tirthayãtrã* (Pilgrimage): Regularly visit holy persons, temples,
   and sacred pilgrimage sites. Such journeys provide freedom from
   routine life and thereby freshen the mind. Pilgrimages also help to
   create a sense of togetherness in the family, since all members
   undertake the pilgrimages together.

3. *Utsava* (Holy Days): Participate in festivals and holy days in the
   home and temple. Observe fasts on holy days. This practice
   inculcates God-consciousness, refreshes the mind and creates a
   sense of togetherness in the family and the community. Hindu
   sages tell us that occasional fasting prevents bodily diseases,
   restores the body's healing power, and heals the mind by
   removing lust, anger, hatred, pride, and jealousy.

4. *Samskãras* (Sacraments): Perform various *Samskãras* in accordance with the scriptures. *Samskãras* are the religious ceremonies
   which mark and sanctify an individual's passage through life.
   They purify the mind by inculcating truthfulness in the mind, and
   purity and generosity in the heart.

5. *Sarva Brahmã* (God is in all): God lives in the hearts of all
   beings. Practice this truth, realize it and be free.

Chapter 11

Chapter 12

Why is Hindu Dharma a Universal Religion?

A religion is universal if its appeal is not restricted to any particular segment of humanity, religious group, nation, race, class, country or age. All religions have some universal aspects, but all aspects of Hindu Dharma are universal. The reason for this difference is that Hindu Dharma does not derive its authority from the teachings of a single person or a book. The spiritual experiences of numerous sages and saints of yore form the basic foundation of Hindu Dharma. A true spiritual experience is always rooted in the universal vision of mankind. The mystics of all religions have invariably held that beyond the apparent diversity of the physical phenomena, there is a perfect unity.

Thousands of years ago, the *rishis* discovered two basic universal principles: the spiritual oneness of all things and beings in the world and the divine nature of the human being. The scholars tell us that Hindu sages were the first to conceive of a true Infinite, from which nothing is excluded. Thus, from its very inception, the foundation of Hindu Dharma was cast into the bedrock of universalism. The following major doctrines, which are central to Hindu beliefs and practices, depict the universal vision of Hindus:

◆ **World Brotherhood**: The most daring universal hypothesis man has ever conceived is the great Upanishadic doctrine *"Aham Brahmasmi,"* meaning "I am the Infinite, the very Infinite from which the universe proceeds." This doctrine identifies every human being—regardless of race, religion, color, sex, or geographic location—with divinity and lays foundation for world

81

brotherhood. Hindu sages have declared that no one is superior or inferior to others. Our individual past karmas have created us as unique individuals. But our differences are temporary and exist only at the physical level. All differences vanish when one attains self-knowledge through a spiritual experience.

♦ **Harmony of Religions**: One of Hindu religion's greatest gifts to mankind is the attitude of religious harmony. Hindus declare that "holiness, purity and charity are not the exclusive possessions of any particular religion in the world and that every system has produced men and women of the most illustrious character." The Hindu scriptures declare, "As the different streams having their sources in different places all mingle their waters in the sea, so, O Lord, the different paths which men take through their tendencies, various though they appear, crooked or straight, all lead to Thee."

♦ **Reasoned Faith**: Hindus declare that blind faith and dogma are the two most vicious sources of conflict in the world; only reasoned faith can ensure harmony in the world. "I know that I myself owe it to thinking that I was able to retain my faith in religion...," writes Dr. Albert Schweitzer.[17] One's deepest convictions must be vindicated by reason.   Reason says that it is irreligious to perform religious actions which cause pain and discomfort to others. It is alright if an organized religion inspires its followers in the existence of God and prescribes a discipline to reach Him. At the same time, it is also important to recognize that God is above all religious systems, even though theologians may set limits to Him.

♦ **Ahimsā (Non-violence)**: Without a true spirit of non-violence towards all forms of life, there can be no genuine peace in the world. For universal harmony, the individual and social actions of people and the economic and political actions of nations must be based upon the attitude of non-violence. In the words of Geoffrey Hodson, a twentieth century theosophical writer, ahimsā is "not mere negative non-injury, [but] positive cosmic love."

"Non-violence is the law of our species as violence is the law of the brute," says Mahatma Gandhi. "The spirit lies dormant in the brute and he knows no law but that of physical might.... Non-violence is the greatest force at the disposal of mankind. It is mightier than the mightiest weapon of destruction devised by the ingenuity of man. Destruction is not the law of the humans....Every murder or other injury, no matter of what cause, committed or inflicted on another, is a crime against humanity." [15,18]

♦ **Universal Prayers**: one of the notable features of Hindu religion is the universality of its prayers. When a Hindu prays, he does not pray for wealth and riches for himself, his family or his community. Instead he prays for enlightening the intellect (to ward off fanaticism) and for the welfare of all the people of the world. This is evident from the following popular prayers that millions of Hindus sing daily in the morning and evening in their home shrines and temples throughout the world:

> *"Asato mã sad gamayo; tamaso mã jyotir gamaya; mrtyor mã amrutum gamaya; Om, shãntih, shãntih, shãntih."* (Brihadãranyaka Upanishad 1.3.28)
>
> "Lead me from unreal to the real; lead me from darkness to light; lead me from death to eternal life. Om, Peace, peace, peace be unto us and all the beings of the world."

> *"Om sarve bhavantu sukhinah, sarve santu nirã-maya-ah; sarve bhadrani pashyantu mã-kaschit dukha-bhak bhavet. Om, shãntih, shãntih, shãntih."*
>
> "Oh Lord, may all [entire mankind] be happy; may all be healthy; may all experience prosperity; may none (in the world) suffer. May peace, peace, peace be unto us and all the beings of the world."

Referring to the above prayer, Arthur Schopenhauer says, "I know of no more beautiful prayer than that [of] the Hindus...'May all that have life be delivered from suffering!'" (Refer to page 71 for another splendid Hindu prayer, *Gãyatrî Mantra*.)

Chapter 13
Hindu View of Ecology

Hindu religion's reverence for the sea, soil, forests, rivers, mountains, plants, birds, and animals stems from its broader view of divinity. Unlike many other religions, Hindus believe that all things and beings in the world are various manifestations of the Ultimate Reality (Brahman), and nothing exists apart from It. The whole emphasis of Hindu scriptures is that human beings cannot separate themselves from nature.

Thousands of years ago, Hindu sages realized that preservation of the environment and ecological balance were necessary for the survival of mankind. To create an awareness among the common people for preservation of the environment, the *rishis* taught that earth has the same relationship with man as a mother with her child. In the Vedic literature, the earth is addressed as Mother Earth and personified as the goddess *Bhumi*, or *Prithvi*. Five thousand years later the world experts addressed earth as Mother Earth for the first time at the Global Conference in 1992 in Rio de Janeiro.

There are numerous direct and indirect messages contained in Hindu scriptures for the protection of our environment and the maintenance of ecological balance. The following are a few examples of some of these timeless teachings: [19]

♦ "One who plants one peepal, one *neem*, ten flowering plants or creepers, two pomegranates, two oranges, and five mangoes does not go to hell." (Varaha Purãna, a Hindu scripture)

♦ "Oh wicked person! If you roast a bird, then your bathing in the sacred rivers, pilgrimage, worship and yagñas are useless."

♦ "The rivers are the veins of God, the ocean is His blood, and the trees the hairs of His body. The air is His breath, the earth His flesh, the sky His abdomen, the hills and mountains the stacks of His bones, and the passing ages are His movements." (Srimad Bhāgavatam 2.1.32-33)

♦ "One should not throw urine, stool or mucus into the water, nor anything mixed with these unholy substances, nor blood or poison, nor any other [impurity]." (Manu Smriti 4.56)

♦ "Five sorts of kindness are the daily sacrifice of the trees. To families they give fuel; to passers by they give shade and a resting place; to birds they give shelter; with their leaves, roots, and bark they give medicines." (Varaha Purāna 162.41-42)

Conclusions

⇨ Feeling one with nature is the fundamental environmental message of Hindu culture. Unlike many other religions, Hindus perceive life not only in human beings, but also in plants, birds, and animals. This vision of oneness of life has helped Hindus develop a worshipful attitude towards everything in nature.

⇨ Nature is not a commodity to be dominated and conquered. Man must change the attitude of dominating nature to one of cooperating with it. A fundamental reorientation of human consciousness is required to recognize that earth has the same relationship with man as a mother with her child.

⇨ Life is an organic entity and the sea, soil, mountains, plants, and animals are inseparable parts of the cosmic web. Man must learn to live in harmony with nature and recognize that plants and animals have a meaningful life too in the cosmic play (*līlā*).

⇨ Environmental issues require a spiritual response. An awareness of the ecological balance must be created at all levels of human thought and activity.

Chapter 13

Chapter 14
Some Philosophical Aspects of Hindu Political, Legal and Economic Thought

The Hindu political, legal and economic thought is included in the *Mahābhārata, Dharma-Shāstras* (of which *Manu-Smriti,* hereafter Manu, is the most important), *Nīti-shāstras* or the science of state-craft (of which the *Shukra-nīti-sāra,* hereafter Shukra, is the most elaborate), and *Artha-shāstras* (of which Kautilya's *Artha-shāstra* is the most popularly available today). The following ideals summarize some of the ancient Hindu views of the political, legal and economic systems which evolved in India over several thousand years:

♦ Man is potentially divine, but is the victim of his ignorance, passions and immoral tendencies, created by his own past actions (*karma*). An ethical and just state is necessary to help man to overcome his sinful and immoral tendencies. "If the king [state] did not vigilantly inflict punishment on the guilty, the stronger would have roasted the weaker like fish." (Manu 7.2)

♦ *Dharma* (morality or righteousness) is the cornerstone of a just and equitable state. *Dharma* preserves the individuals and the society. The oft-quoted axiom is: "Hunger, sleep, fear, and sex are common to all animals, human and sub-human. It is the additional attribute of *dharma* that differentiates man from the beast." Thus, the political philosophy (*danda-nīti*) of the state must be grounded in *dharma.* In ancient literature, the righteous king (state) is believed to be *dharma* itself, created by God for the protection of all beings. (Manu 7.3 and 7.14).

- In personal life *dharma* is expressed as virtues and duties. In the political life *dharma* is expressed as the just and equitable laws which restrain evil and promote virtuous life. In the Hindu polity, politicians are required to inspire virtue and loyalty to the laws of the state by their own examples. In Hindu legal literature the word *dharma* conveys the same meaning as the words *ethical, reasonable,* and *equitable* in Western legal literature.

- *Dharma* (morality), *artha* (wealth), *kāma* (enjoyment), and *moksha* (spiritual perfection) constitute the four ends (*catur varga*) of Hindu religious life. However, both the Mahābhārata Shāntiparva 15.3 and Manu 2.224 include only *dharma, artha* and *kāma* as the three basic values (*tri-varga)* on which social and political philosophy should be founded upon.

- Since ancient times Hindus have recognized that since *moksha,* and the paths leading to it, differ from one religious path to another, the state must not interfere with an individual's spiritual life. At the same time, the state must not allow violation of the basic laws of morality. Thus, Hindu tradition demands strict social morality, but provides freedom of thought and choice in ultimate matters. This forms the basis for the consistent pattern of the secular outlook of Hindus in religious, social and political matters all throughout their history.

- Hindu social thought rejects the views that *dharma* alone, or *dharma* and wealth alone, or wealth and enjoyment alone are the most important values for human life. The predominant view of Hindu social thought is that all three values (dharma, wealth, and enjoyment) must be harmoniously cultivated for pursuit of happiness. (Manu 2.224)

- The assignment of duties should be in accordance with merit and the ability to perform the work (*guna-karma*) (Shukra 1.38). The foundation of an ethical state depends upon the selection of honest and efficient administrators and their level of training in particular jobs.

Chapter 14

♦ "The king [state] should behave in three different ways: like the [pleasant] autumn moon to the learned, like the [scorching] summer sun to the enemy, and like the [moderate] spring sun to the subjects." (Shukra 2.282)

♦ Harmlessness is the highest *dharma*, but for protection of life, property, and *dharma*, the state may resort to violence, if necessary under given circumstances. (Mahābhārata Shānti-parva, 15). "I would rather have India resort to arms in order to defend her honor than that she should, in a cowardly manner, become or remain a helpless witness to her own dishonor," declares Mahatma Gandhi, the apostle of peace.

♦ The Hindu system of justice stresses that the persons administering justice should be knowledgeable in the methods of logic as described in the *Nyāya* school of Hindu philosophy. *Nyāya* includes methodology based on logic to evaluate arguments and/or evidence for and against a defendant in order to ascertain the truth. An unimpeachable character, knowledge of the law, training, and knowledge of logic are the basic requirements for the administration of justice.

♦ Capital punishment violates the Vedic injunction against taking any life. (Shukra 4.1.92-108)

♦ Both Manu and Shukra prescribe heavier punishment for those in higher social positions and who violate their duties. "Where an ordinary person is fined one coin, a judge should be fined one thousand coins." (Manu 8.326)

♦ The right to life logically leads to the right to wealth, since wealth is needed for the maintenance of life itself. *Dharma* provides the ethical means for earning one's wealth.

Conclusions

⇨ The ancient Hindu political, legal and economic theories point to a continued tradition of a strong central government under a king (state). The authority of the government was vested in a council of ministers, who were selected based on their character and merit. *Dharma* was the cornerstone of the political and social theories of ancient India.

⇨ The village was the unit of the ancient Hindu society. Village life was viewed very favorably, as is clear from the saying, "It is impossible for one to attain salvation who lives in a town covered with dust." [25]

⇨ The Hindu instinct that goodness and virtue warrant sympathy and reconciliation with other forms of thought and belief is best expressed in the following words: "The greatest contribution to posterity made by the Hindu tradition was the broad-mindedness, sympathy, and tolerance of different viewpoints exhibited almost alone in India amongst the civilized communities of earlier day.[25]

⇨ "When Egypt persecuted the Jews, when racial and communal conflicts disfigured the history of Babylon and Nineveh, when, later on, we see that the slave states in Greece and Rome formed the basis of those marvelous cultures, and when in medieval ages the baiting of Jews alternated with the baiting of Roman Catholics by Protestants and vice versa, we had the spectacle in India of unfailing hospitality to foreign religions and foreign cultures." [25]

⇨ "What country can show anything like the treatment of the Parsees, who, flying from oppression in their own country of Persia, asked for and obtained succor of the wise west-coast king [in India], to whose protection and active encouragement of their faith and tradition the Parsees ultimately owe their dominant position in India today?" [25]

⇨ Hindus say, "*samavāya eva sādhuh*," meaning "Concord is the supreme good." Thousands of years ago, Hindu sages declared that *dharma* (righteousness), *ahimsā* (non-violence), *dayā* (compassion), *abhaya* (fearlessness) and recognition of the unity of existence are the supreme virtues for mankind. Today these ideals form the fundamental charter of the United Nations organization.

Chapter 14

Chapter 15
Hindu Response to Modern Problems

Individuality is the result of association of *ātman* (spirit) with a human body. A human body without ātman is a dead body and ātman without a human body cannot manifest itself in the phenomenal world. Thus individual personality comprises of two components, physical and spiritual. Because of this natural constitution of the human personality, human happiness depends upon balanced fulfillment of the spiritual and physical needs of one's being.

The scientific and technological revolution of the twentieth century has provided man with substantial amenities of life. We have made immense progress in fulfilling our physical needs. However, we have ignored our spiritual needs and the result is catastrophic. The break-ups in families resulting in children with single parents or no parents, child abuse, spousal abuse, teenage pregnancy, drugs, violence and crime have increased to epidemic levels in modern affluent societies. The root cause of all these problems is that we are focusing our full attention on the physical needs alone and no attention on the spiritual needs. We have become very materialistic in our outlook and in the process lost our souls.

Cosmos is One Family (*Vasudhaiva Kutumbakam*)

In the past several centuries, science and technology have presented to us a mechanistic world view which defines the world as an aggregate of particles of matter. This mechanistic view of the world has led human beings to evaluate all political, economic, environmental, and social issues in a fragmentary way. This fragmented world view presents a separate existence for each unit without any relationship with other beings, nature and God. Thus a modern human being tries to resolve problems with a specialized view which is only a partial view.

Thousands of years ago, sages discovered that all things and beings of the universe are the manifestation of the Supreme Self. "All are in One and One is in all," the sages declared. The sages described the creation as a continuous, dynamic, and blissful experience. The modern scientific view is still short of experiencing the blissful aspect of Reality. Recent developments in physics have shown that there are no definite boundaries separating the fundamental particles, the building blocks of matter, from one another. The scientists observing these particles and the instruments of observation are part of a continuous stream of energy. The current world view of the unconnected existence of everything in creation is at the root of many of our modern problems. The so-called freedom of the human beings is grossly misunderstood as is evident from the uncontrolled expressions of human behavior and controlled thought processes by political interests and religious dogmas.

The fragmented view of life has distorted the relationship of individuals, families, societies, nature and God. The realizations of the ancient seers found the entire cosmos to be one family. Every aspect of creation was seen as the expression of the same eternal principle described as Brahman, God or Ultimate Truth.

Systems Must Unfold the Divinity of Human Beings

In modern societies success is measured by possessions, positions and power. Scientific knowledge has been exploited to control the external nature without any attention to the control of the inner nature. This modern paradigm of success misses the important parameter of character. The foundation of human life is character, the moral and ethical ability of an individual to respond to the external conditions of life. In ancient wisdom, the emphasis was on the integrity of body, mind, intellect and soul.

The sages taught that every child that is born owes *Three Debts* that must be repaid in the adult life. First, there is a debt to God that one can repay by dedicating one's life to the service of God. To a

Hindu, service of God means service to all mankind, regardless of caste, color or creed. Service of God also includes reverence for parents, teachers, the practice of non-violence, and truthfulness, a pleasant and respectful attitude toward others, especially elders, obeying scriptural injunctions, and practice of self-control and purity of thought. In Hindu culture, respect and reverence for old age is recognized as partial repayment of this first debt to God.

A second debt is to the sages and saints who have revealed the truths in the Vedas and other scriptures. This debt can be paid off by serving sages, saints, and gurus and by preserving and enriching the cultural heritage that is handed down through each generation. In the absence of sages and saints in modern societies, the repayment of this debt involves contributing generously, without desire for reward, for the benefit of the needy, homeless, handicapped, sick, poor, and less fortunate.

The third debt is to one's ancestors which includes raising one's family in accordance with the moral and ethical principles of dharma. To enable an individual to fulfill both the physical and spiritual needs, the ancient sages organized life into four stages: studentship, householder, retirement and renunciation. The three main goals of the studentship stage of life are to acquire knowledge, build one's character, and learn to shoulder responsibilities that will fall upon the individual during his (or her) adult life. This stage begins when a child enters school at an early age and continues until he has finished all schooling and is prepared to assume the responsibilities of the future.

The student is expected to acquire two types of knowledge. First, he must acquire knowledge in the arts and sciences, and learn necessary skills for earning a decent living in the world. Second, the individual must acquire religious and spiritual knowledge, the moral and ethical principles of dharma. He must learn to discipline the body and mind, practice self-restraint, non-violence, and truthfulness.

The householder stage begins with one's marriage, which in Hindu way of life is regarded as a sacrament, and not a social contract. This stage forms the foundation for the support of the other two stages that follow. The importance of the householder stage is often reflected in the analogy that just as all rivers flow into the sea, all stages flow into the householder stage.

An individual's competence in successfully assuming the duties and responsibilities of the householder stage of life depends upon the intensity and the depth of knowledge acquired during the studentship stage. During the householder stage an individual pays the *Three Debts*. A householder earns wealth and enjoys good and noble things in life in accordance with the formula *dharma-artha-kama*—refer to the discussion of Four Ends in Chapter 5.

After the responsibilities of the householder stage are complete (i.e., one's children have reached adulthood and have assumed the responsibilities), one enters the retirement stage, known as the ascetic or hermit stage of life. In this stage one gradually withdraws from active life and begins devoting more time to the study of scriptures, contemplation and meditation. The individual, however, makes himself available in order to provide guidance and share experiences with the younger generation, when requested to do so.

The renunciation stage is the final stage of life in which an individual mentally renounces all worldly ties, spends all of his time in meditation and contemplation and ponders over the mysteries of life. In this stage of life an individual must forgo the concepts of *I*, *My*, or *Mine*, and evolve his or her consciousness to seek oneness of all existence. In ancient times one would part company with one's family and meditate in a forest. In modern societies this stage can be regarded as complete mental renunciation of the world and total absorption in meditation and contemplation.

Excellence is the Goal of Life, Not Competition

Without adequate attention to manifest the divine power that lies dormant within every individual, one is left to suffer when stripped of material prosperity, titles or powers. While competitiveness does enhance individual skills, lack of basic character and human values cannot be replaced by personal skills.

Individuals motivated by the goal of excellence in life strive to bring the best out of their beings without concern for competition with others. The ideal of personal success for completely selfish goals is highly stressful. Greater joy in life can be derived by sharing the fruits of one's work with others. Society's current paradigm of happiness is possessing, hoarding, and thinking of "me" and "my rights." The sages tell us that greater joy arises from sharing, caring, and loving. Nothing feeds the human heart with a sense of satisfaction as much as acts of service to others. The Vedic prayers (see page 83) for the well-being of all living creatures should be the inspiration behind the vision of the harmonious world.

The Paradigm of Happiness is Selflessness and Charity

The competitive lifestyle in modern societies encourages individuals and nations to accumulate more and more wealth and material possessions without regard for the welfare of others. The possessive nature of the mind is one of the major causes of pain, suffering, and injustice in the world today. If actions of individuals and nations were motivated by the instinct of charity, the problems of poverty and starvation could be significantly alleviated. Forms of charity such as Meals on Wheels, planting of trees, and provision of food, clothing and medicines to refugees are all relevant in modern times. Charity basically means sharing what God has given us with all of God's creatures. According to the Bhagavad Gîtâ 3.12, one who takes from the society and does not give back to those in need is a thief.

In Hindu view, charity encompasses a great deal more than giving away money, food or clothing. Charity also includes sharing good thoughts, words and deeds with others. Our prayers and good wishes to others are also expressions of charity. Giving away material gifts fulfills the need of the moment, but giving education, building and maintaining temples and charitable institutions, or serving as volunteers at such establishments plants seeds of hope for the future. Giving to those who are in need, such as the poor, hungry, sick, and homeless helps us in two distinct ways. First, the charitable actions help the ātman to slowly free itself from material bondage and attain union with God. "Liberation is only for he who gives up everything for others. Even the least work done for others awakens the power within; even thinking of the least good of others gradually instills into the heart the strength of a lion," says Swami Vivekānanda.[26,30]

Problem	Cause	Solution
Religious and cultural intolerance, poverty, political and economic exploitation.	Notion of separate identity from each other and from God; mechanistic view of the world.	Recognition of the basic Hindu doctrines of unity of existence and potential divinity of all human beings.
Ethical and moral degradation.	Lack of character; the present system of education allows the mind to gather facts and store and process data before it knows how to control itself.	Educational institutions must install life-building, man-making and character-making systems. Control of the mind should be taught before data acquisition and processing occurs.
Crime and violence	Injustices and inequalities, wrong thinking, fear, indifference, hatred, moral decay, impulse to meet disagreement with force, lack of values and attitudes.	A fundamental change of values and attitudes is required to recognize injustices and inequities in the society. A spiritual response is necessary to ensure true justice and equality among all people.
Family break-ups, unwanted babies, and ill treatment of elders	Non-recognition of the spiritual nature of individuals, fragmentary world view and competitive life styles.	Recognition of the *Three Debts, Four Stages* of life, and striving for excellence and not competition.
Environmental degradation.	Fragmentary world view leading to the irresponsible use of natural resources.	Realization that nature is not a commodity to be dominated and conquered. The planet earth must be treated as Mother Earth.

Table 5

Chapter 15

Secondly, serving others helps us to improve our own health. The authors of the book titled *The Healing Power of Doing Good* researched several thousand volunteer organizations.[31] They concluded that 95 percent of those researched exhibited increased self-esteem, serenity, relaxation and positive sense of well-being. They further concluded that serving others resulted in a significant reduction in stress and stress-related illnesses among the volunteers.

Hindu religious literature describes some specific acts of charity which far exceed the normal standards of compassion. For example:

♥ After being pursued by a hungry vulture, an injured bird fell in the lap of the Great Emperor Sibhi. The emperor cut a part of his own thigh, offered it to the hungry vulture as food, and treated the injured bird.

♥ While traveling in his chariot, a king saw a creeper plant grown over the road. The king left his chariot on the roadside for the creeper plant to climb and grow on the chariot and traveled to his palace on foot.

Hindu Vision of a Harmonious World:

⇨ Where harmlessness to all creatures is the highest culture, service to the poor is the highest worship, compassion is the highest religion, truth is the highest law, and love for all God's creatures is the highest philosophy.

⇨ Where political, social and religious institutions and their leaders strive tirelessly to accept people of all races, colors and creeds, and respect their faiths and beliefs.

⇨ Where all forms of life are revered as various expressions of the Supreme Lord and ahimsã is the governing law.

⇨ Where educational, political and economic systems are designed to assist individuals to unfold their highest potential.

⇨ Where mothers, fathers, teachers and elders are revered, children are brought up with self-esteem, and the young are taught to respect intrinsic human values.

Chapter 16
Contribution of Hindus to the World Culture

From the invention of the decimal system in mathematics to the noble philosophy of ahimsã, Hindus have contributed their share in all fields of knowledge and learning. Over five thousand years ago, when Europeans were only nomadic forest dwellers, ancient Hindus had established a civilization, known as the Harappan culture, in the Indus Valley, the northwestern region of India. When much of the world was still sunk in sleep, people of the Harappan culture were conducting trade workshops in weaving, bead-making, pottery, dying of fabrics, and metallurgy.

The people of the Indus Valley also produced seals, used for documenting business transactions. The seals were made of stone (in the form of square tablets) and were engraved with figures of animals, such as goats, buffalo, elephants, and tigers. The discovery of these seals in distant lands suggests that the Harappan navigators must have sailed as far as Mesopotamia for trade. Most of the knowledge that ancient Hindus had acquired in the fields of arts and sciences passed onto Egypt and subsequently to Greece and Europe. In the words of Georges Ifrah, "Still more important was the influence of Indian astronomers, from whom they [Arabs] borrowed, probably beginning in the eighth century, their zero, decimal-place-value numeration, and computation methods." [28]

In his *Dictionary of Scholars*, Ali ibn-Yusuf al-Qifti, a Moslem scholar (1172-1248), wrote, "there came from India to Baghdad a man deeply learned in the doctrines of his country. This man knew the method of *sindhid* [an Arabic transcription of the Sanskrit *siddhãnta*, "astronomical cannon"], concerning the movements of the heavenly bodies and equations calculated by means of trigonometric ratios in quarters of a degree. He also knew various ways of determining eclipses and the risings of the signs of the zodiac. He had composed a summary of a work on these subjects, attributed to a prince named Figar. In it, the *kardagas* were calculated by minutes. The *caliph* [king] ordered that the Indian treatise be translated into Arabic, to help Moslems acquire exact knowledge of the stars. The translation was done by Mohammed ibn-Ibrahim al-Fazzari, the first Moslem to have made a thorough study of astronomy." [28]

A discussion of some of the other achievements of the ancient Hindus is summarized below:

♦ The world's first university was established at Takshashila (northwest region of India) in approximately 700 BCE. Another large university was established at Nalanda around 500 AD. According to the Chinese traveler Hieun Tsang, the campus housed 10,000 students, 2,000 professors, and a large administrative staff.

♦ Ancient Hindus provided the concept of zero to the world. In early Sanskrit texts and in Pangala's Chandra Sutra (200 AD), "zero" is called Shunya. Later, Bhaskarācharya (400-500 AD) showed that any number divided by zero becomes infinity and infinity divided by any number remains infinity. Zero is also described by Brahmaguptā in his famous seventh century work, called Brahma Bhuta Siddhanta. Later, zero appeared in Arabic books in 770 AD and from there it was carried to Europe in 800 AD.

♦ In addition to the concept of zero, the place-value system, the decimal system was developed in India as early as 100 BCE. Ancient Hindus had also developed prefixes for raising ten to powers as high as fifty-three. "The Indian place-value numeration with zero sign ranks among humanity's fundamental discoveries. Through the centuries it has been propagated even more widely than the alphabet of Phoenician origin, and it has now become the only real universal language. When the advantages became apparent to the scholars and reckoners of civilizations in contact with India, they gradually abandoned the imperfect systems transmitted to them by their ancestors." [28]

♦ Pi, the ratio of the circumference of a circle to its diameter, is stated to be approximately equal to three in the 600 BCE Sanskrit text Baudhayana Sulba Sutra. In 497 AD, Aryabhatta calculated the value of pi as 3.146, as a ratio of 62832/2000.

♦ Pythagoras is credited with the invention of the Pythagorean Theorem in 500 BCE. According to this theorem the square of the hypotenuse of a right-angled triangle equals the sum of the squares of the two sides. However, this theorem was developed by the Hindu mathematician Baudhayana one hundred years earlier in 600 BCE. In his book Baudhayana Sulba Sutra (600 BCE), Baudhayana states, "The area produced by the diagonal [i.e. the area of the square formed by the diagonal] of a right-angled triangle is equal to the sum of the areas produced by it on two sides [i.e. the sum of the areas of the squares formed by its two sides]."

♦ In Surya Siddhanta, dated 400-500 AD, the ancient Hindu astronomer Bhaskaracharya states, "Objects fall on the earth due to a force of attraction by the earth. Therefore, the earth, planets, constellations, moon, and sun are held in orbit due to this force." Approximately 1200 years later (1687 AD), Sir Isaac Newton rediscovered this phenomenon and called it the Law of Gravity.

♦ In his treatise *Aryabhateeyam*, dated 500 AD, the Hindu genius Aryabhatta states, "Just as a person traveling in a boat feels that the trees on the bank are moving, people on the earth feel that the sun is moving." He also explains that the earth is round, rotates on its axis, orbits the sun, and is suspended in space. The lunar and solar eclipses are further explained by Aryabhatta as the interplay of the shadows of the sun, moon, and the earth.

♦ According to modern calculations, the time taken by the earth to orbit the sun is 365.2596 days. In Surya Siddhanta, dated 400-

500 AD, Bhaskarãcharya calculated this time as 365.258756484 days.

♦ Ayur Veda, or "the science of life," is the traditional system of Indian medicine that originated from the fourth book of Vedic literature, the Atharva Veda. This system of medicine, developed in 1000-500 BCE, uses natural herbs to cure diseases, and is still used in India and many other countries of the world.

♦ The Greek physician Hippocrates (460-377 BCE) is honored as the father of medicine. However, well before Hippocrates, Maharshi Charaka had already written the Charaka Samhitã ("Handbook of a Physician") in 500 BCE.

♦ The earliest known work relating to human surgery is Shushruta Samhitã, written in approximately 600 BCE by the Hindu surgeon Shushruta, who performed plastic surgery as early as 600 BCE. Chanakya's Arthashãstra describes post-mortems, and Bhoja Prabandha describes brain surgery, successfully performed in 927 AD by two surgeons on King Bhoja to remove a growth from his brain.

♦ The game of chess was developed in India and was originally called *Astapada* (sixty-four squares). Later this game came to be known as *Chaturanga* (four corps). In 600 AD this game was learned by Persians who named it Shatranj (derived from the original word *Chaturanga*).

♦ The science of yoga originated from the Vedas. Today many variations of Hatha Yoga, in the form of a system of exercises, are used in many countries for the preservation and growth of the human body.

♦ Hinduism has given the world the wisdom of the Vedas, the Upanishads, and the Bhagavad Gîtã. Free from any kind of dogma, Hindu scriptures teach universal harmony, self-dignity, and reverence for all forms of life. "All mankind is one family," is the slogan of Hindu sages.

Chapter 16

◆ Sanskrit (meaning "cultured"), the classical language of Hinduism, is the oldest and the most systematic language in the world. The vastness, versatility, and power of expression of Sanskrit can be appreciated by the fact that this language has 65 words to describe various forms of earth, 67 words for water, and over 250 words to describe various types of rainfall. According to Forbes magazine (July, 1987), "Sanskrit is the most convenient language for computer software programming."

◆ The glory of the Sanskrit literature is described by Juan Mascaro, an eminent linguist and Sanskrit scholar, "Sanskrit literature is a great literature. We have the great songs of the Vedas, the splendor of the Upanishads, the glory of the Bhagavad Gîtã, the vastness (100,000 verses) of the Mahãbhãrata, the tenderness and the heroism found in the Rãmãyana, the wisdom of the fables and stories of India, the scientific philosophy of Sankhya, the psychological philosophy of yoga, the poetical philosophy of Vedanta, the Laws of Manu, the grammar of Panini and other scientific writings, and the lyrical poetry and dramas of Kãlidãsa. Sanskrit literature, on the whole, is a romantic literature interwoven with idealism and practical wisdom, and with a passionate longing for spiritual vision." [21]

◆ Panini's Sanskrit grammar, produced in about 300 BCE, is the shortest and the fullest grammar in the world. According to Sir Monier-Williams (Eng. Sanskrit scholar, 1819-1899): "The Panini grammar reflects the wondrous capacity of the human brain, which till today no other country has been able to produce except India."

◆ The sacred syllable AUM (ॐ), believed to be the sound of creation, when correctly intoned (recited), is said to include all sounds of music and associated rhythms. The Vedic hymns are metrical and were recited in music over five thousand years ago. The Sama Veda is the source of Indian classical music, which is heavily rooted in spiritualism. Indian music is not only a melody, but an experience in the unity of the body, mind, and spirit.

Chapter 17
Practicing Hindu Dharma in Foreign Lands

Practicing Hindu Dharma in foreign lands presents an opportunity and a challenge as well as a dilemma. Modern emphasis on the materialistic aspects of human life has created a spiritual vacuum in affluent societies of the world. The lack of a spiritual vision of life is taking a heavy toll on moral, ethical, family and human values. Apprehension, anxiety and daily worries about one's job, material needs of the present, and financial security for the future in a "cut-throat" competitive environment is causing confusion regarding the basic purpose of life.

The current confusion of affluent societies is similar to that of Arjuna in the Mahābhārata war. Arjuna, with all his sophisticated weapons and military might, represents the scientific and techno-logical advancement of the modern world. Krishna, who gave spiritual instruction to Arjuna and removed his (Arjuna's) confusion, represents the spiritual force needed to resolve the restlessness, worries and confusion in today's world. Vision and action must be blended every step of the way to bring harmony in human life. Where Krishna and Arjuna are together, therein lies the opportunity for progress and ultimate victory.

The challenge to practicing Hindu Dharma (or for that matter any other religion) in modern societies arises largely due to the illusion of rationality. This illusion leads to the view that nothing is real if it cannot be directly or indirectly perceived by the senses. We also tend to believe that reason is highest in man and that it can give us a reliable and complete understanding of all our problems.

The sages tell us that intuition is the result of direct knowledge of Truth and thus intuition is superior to and transcends reason. A reasonable man is not necessarily a virtuous man. In today's world reason is often used to separate rather than unite people. The sages further tell us that faith and devotion are the powerful tools which can be used to tread a spiritual path until one gains intuition through one's own spiritual experience.

Owing to the increased scientific and technological outlook in modern societies, the traditional methods of religious teaching based upon mythology, ritualism, and folk religion are losing their power. The questions that are being raised by the younger generation pose a dilemma for those who rely solely on mythological, ritualistic and sociological forms to provide basis for their beliefs and practices.

In the Mahābhārata war Krishna did not use mythology, ritualism or folk religion to address Arjuna's concerns pertaining to his role in the war.   Instead, Krishna used ancient philosophical thought to answer Arjuna's numerous queries.   It was the power of the philosophical teachings of the Vedas and Upanishads that inspired Arjuna to address his final words to Krishna, "Destroyed is my delusion, Oh Krishna. I stand firm with my doubts dispelled. I shall act according to Thy word." (BG 18.73).

Practicing Hindu Dharma means combining devotion, knowledge and work—love, light and life—for the benefit of one's family, society, country, and the world, with the ultimate goal of union with God. The following guidelines are intended to accomplish this goal by blending the vision of Hindu Dharma with the actions of individuals and social institutions:

♦ Establish a temple room (or a corner in a room, if the entire room is not available) for daily worship and meditation. Install a family deity—a picture, image or a symbol—in the temple room and worship the deity daily in the morning and evening. Perform the daily routine as described in Chapter 11.

♦ Have a firm conviction that the family deity will protect and aid if sincere prayers, offerings and vows are made regularly with love and devotion.   Paramahamsa Sri Rāmakrishna is a modern example of how high one can rise spiritually by sincerely performing deity worship alone.

♦ Meditate daily and practice yogic exercises regularly. In order to successfully live in this world of "cut-throat" competition, one requires a healthy body and a strong mind. Meditation strengthens the mind and yoga preserves the body.

♦ Meditation and yoga are the backbone of Hindu religious and cultural tradition. Establish yoga and meditation centers and libraries to learn and practice the philosophical and theological themes of Hindu Dharma.

♦ Earnestly organize and support temple activities to preserve the traditional religious and cultural heritage. Donate generously to temples and community service organizations.

♦ Organize, support, coordinate or host religious festivals and celebrations of birthdays of saints, sages and holy men and women.

♦ Organize conferences, seminars, symposiums, discussions, and debates at temples, community centers, and educational institutions to expound the teachings of the scriptures and to illustrate how the spiritual wisdom of Hindu sages and saints can be utilized to solve problems facing the modern world. Ahimsã, the divinity of ãtman, and unity of existence are the three jewels of ancient wisdom which can promote unity and harmony in the divided world of today. In the words of Donald H. Bishop, Professor of Philosophy at Washington State University, "A major contribution [that] Indian thought can make today is to remind the world of the illusions it must overcome. Our present crisis results from living by illusions. Indian thought would call us back to the real." [22]

♦ Invite saints, swamis and scholars to provide discourses on religious and spiritual topics of interest.

♦ Support, participate and organize pilgrimages.

♦ Support, organize and participate in weekly religious activities, such as *bhajans*, *kirtans*, and scriptural readings (*swadhyaya*).

Chapter 17

◆ Organize events and activities of common interest to enhance the spirit of unity in the community and pride in the Hindu way of life, and to foster friendship and understanding between Hindu Americans and other Americans.

◆ Establish cultural centers to promote religious and cultural activities. Promote media activities such as radio, television and newspapers to expound the true teachings of Hindu Dharma and to clarify misunderstandings or misinformation about Hindu religious teachings.

◆ Raise, collect and disseminate funds for charity work within the Hindu community, other communities, the country, and the world.

◆ Educated Hindus need a demythologized and less ritualistic Hindu Dharma to blend modernity with the vision of the Vedas, Upanishads and other Hindu scriptures. In addition to normal activities, temples need to raise funds to support various institutions such as universities, yoga and meditation centers, senior citizen centers, and hospitals. Such institutions would be the symbol and model of the modern Hindu Dharma.

◆ Organize and support dramatic pageants based on the Purãnic and Epic literature. These pageants carry traditional religious ideals to the young generation and are effective tools of popular religious instruction for modern societies.

◆ Hindu festivals, art, music and dance are the four pillars of Hindu culture. Organize and support these activities regularly. Such events should be used to foster friendship and promote understanding between Hindus and other communities.

◆ Remember "He who sees Shiva [God] in the poor, in the weak, and in the diseased, really worships Shiva; and if he sees Shiva only in the image, his worship is but preliminary. He who has served and helped one poor man, seeing Shiva in him, without thinking of his caste, creed or race, or anything, with him Shiva is more pleased than with the man who sees him only in temples," declares Swami Vivekananda.[30]

Chapter 17

Chapter 18
Timeless Wisdom for Today's Youth

As a youth, you are the architect of your own destiny. What you are today is in part the result of what you have been thinking and doing in the past. What you think and do today will determine your tomorrow. The following guidelines from ancient wisdom will inspire you to live a purposeful life.

Purpose of Human Life
The purpose of human life is to unfold one's inner potential. You are neither a body-mind apparatus nor a limited individual. You are in reality *ātman* living in a physical body. The body and mind are simply the media to manifest your inner potential in this lifetime. Your limitations are the limitations of the body and not of the *ātman*. The mind, being the reflection of the *ātman*, possesses tremendous power, which must be developed and manifested. Mahatma Gandhi is an example of what a person with even a weak physical body but a strong mind can achieve in one lifetime.

Set Goals
Always remember that a life without goals is akin to a journey without destination. The four ends (i.e. general goals) of human life are to develop virtue (*dharma*), acquire wealth (*artha)*, fulfill desires (*kama*) and attain spiritual perfection (*moksha*). Therefore, acquiring diploma(s), becoming married, having children and supporting them through college, growing old, and dying are not really the goals; these are merely a few toll-booths on the highway of human life. You must establish specific goals to unfold your own inner potential.

Important Tools

The head, heart and hands are the three important tools needed to accomplish one's goals. These tools must be perfected during youthful years and properly coordinated later in adult life to achieve success. To sharpen the head, you must acquire education in arts and sciences and learn necessary technical skills to help you make a decent living in this world. As part of the overall education, you must learn the spiritual principles of life, read scriptures and study the lives of sages, saints, and great men and women of the world. To kindle the lamp of your heart, you need to develop qualities such as love, non-violence, kindness, and compassion. To strengthen hands, you must maintain a healthy body. Proper diet and regular exercises such as simple *Hatha Yoga* and *Pranayama* exercises can be used to permanently maintain the physical body in a healthy state. [30]

Build Your Character

"What the world today needs is character," says Vivekãnanda. A man without character is like a wild bull let loose in a cornfield. Every fool may become a hero at one time or another, but the people of good character are heroes all the time. Establishing good character means acquiring established wisdom (*pratishthita prajna*). Nothing great can be achieved in life without a good character.

The character of an individual is the aggregate of his mental tendencies. If good tendencies prevail, the character becomes good and if evil tendencies prevail, the character becomes evil. When an individual performs good work and continuously thinks virtuous thoughts, there is an irresistible force in him to be good and to do good. One's good character is said to be established when one is under complete control of his good tendencies.

We live by our habits and habit is the "second nature" of man. One's character is essentially a pattern of repeated habits. Therefore, develop good habits. Be aware of your habits at all times and counteract bad habits with better ones. Value time and be punctual. Never think, "It does not matter if I arrive on time when everyone else comes half-an-hour late." It does matter, since you are the one who can set an example for everyone else. As they say, "two wrongs don't make a right."

Time management is a critical factor for success in today's world. Since you cannot do everything that crosses your mind, prioritize your work. Develop the habit of using things-to-do lists to help you perform the daily chores around the house and at the work-place or wherever you may be.

Develop an Integrated Personality

To be successful in life, you must develop a well-balanced personality. Yoga, devotion, knowledge and action are the four components of an integrated personality. These are akin to the four wheels of an automobile. If one wheel loses air, the automobile cannot be driven too far with only three wheels in operation. A man with great intellect but no feelings cannot do much good to the world. Likewise, a man of great devotion but no action is not useful either. An ideal man would be the one who has the intellect of Shankara, the heart of Buddha, and the body of Arjuna.

Apply the Power of Positive Thinking

God has given us not only the mind and ability to think, but also the choice to create from our thoughts. Thought is the power of the mind that manifests in the things we create. For example, a beautiful statue is not the work of a hammer and chisel, but of the sculptor's thought. The hammer and chisel are the tools that merely remove the excess material so that the sculptor's ideas can be manifested.

Sages tell us that the mind is so powerful that if we think of a particular disease all the time, that disease will appear in the body. Similarly if we think of success all the time, then success will be achieved. Remember that constructive thoughts create our goals and destructive thoughts destroy them. Whatever you harbor in the inner-most chamber of your heart will shape itself sooner or later in the outward life. Since the state of doing comes from thinking, fill the mind with the highest ideals and divine thoughts.

To inspire the mind with divine thoughts anytime and anywhere, imagine yourself soaring high in the sky like a bird and sing the following song mentally or loudly (as birds sing, without caring who listens or what the listeners think):

No birth, no death, no caste, Have I;
limitations have I none.
I am He, I am He, blessed spirit I am He.
Freedom I don't care, bondage I don't fear
I am free, ever free, I am He, I am He.
I am He, I am He, blessed spirit I am He.

According to sages, regular divine affirmations eliminate physical and mental restlessness, worries and anger, and provide inner strength to face the challenges of life. The following affirmations have been recommended by Paramahansa Yogānanda for daily use. Deep and persistent repetition of these affirmations will help you to express the power of positive thinking to overcome physical, mental and spiritual obstacles.

"God's perfect health permeates the dark nooks of my bodily sickness. In all my cells His healing light is shining. They are entirely well, for His perfection is in them." [24]

"I possess the creative power of Spirit. The infinite intelligence will guide me and solve every problem." [24]

Have Faith in Yourself
One of the most important prerequisites for success is to have faith in oneself. If you don't have faith in your own self, you are essentially denying expression to the soul-power that is hidden within you. "Not believing in the glory of our own soul is what Vedanta calls atheism....The old religion said that he was an atheist who did not believe in God. The new religion says that he is an atheist who does not believe in himself," declares Swāmī Vivekānanda.

Whatever you think is what you are. If you think you are weak and helpless, that is exactly what you are. If you think yourself to be strong, strong you are. No good can possibly come out of a person who thinks himself to be helpless, incompetent or incapable.

The history of the world is the history of a few men and women who had faith in themselves. We cannot blame the sun for not giving us light if we choose to shut the doors and windows in a room and live in darkness. Faith in yourself and faith (shraddhā) in God is the secret of success, happiness, and greatness in this world.

Be Moderate in Thoughts and Actions

If you want to live a harmonious life, you must learn to be moderate in whatever you do. Extremism of any kind is dangerous to the body, mind and soul. The Bhagavad Gītā declares (BG 6.16-17):

"[success in] Yoga is not for one who eats too much or eats too little, nor for one who sleeps too much or sleeps too little. To one who is moderate in eating, in recreation, in his efforts in work, and sleep and wakefulness, yoga is the destroyer of miseries."

Eat Foods that Revitalize the Mind

In Hindu view, the mind is a material entity and attains intelligence by its proximity with ātman. Being material, the mind consists of a substance which is the essence of the food consumed. According to the Chāndogya Upanishad 6.5.1, the food, when eaten, becomes divided into three parts.[12] The grossest portion of the food consumed is eliminated as waste matter by the organism. The middle portion is transformed into bodily structure, and the subtlest portion serves to build up the mind. "We are what we eat," is the common adage. "Our food and eating habits determine in no small measure our environs and general outlook on life," says Dr. Rajendra Prasad, first president of India. "A man who wants to control his passions does so easily if he controls his palate," says Mahatma Gandhi.

According to the Bhagavad Gītā 17.7-10, foods are of three kinds, sāttvic, rājasic, and tāmasic. Sāttvic foods are sweet, soft and nourishing. They promote life, vitality, strength, health, joy, cheerfulness, and render the mind calm and thoughtful. The sāttvic foods include whole grains, fresh fruits and vegetables, milk, and milk products. Rājasic foods are bitter, sour, saltish, hot, pungent, and very spicy. They produce pain, grief, disease and make the mind restless, unsteady and uncontrollable. The rājasic foods include fish and chicken, spices, tea, coffee, soft drinks, beer and wine. The tãmasic foods are those which are stale, putrid, impure, require lot of energy to digest, and are made of the lifeless matter. They fill the mind with anger, inertia and dullness. The tãmasic foods include red meat (such as beef and veal), deep fried foods, and hard liquor.

Honor Parents, Teachers and Elders

According to Hindu scriptures, God loves, nourishes and cares for you through your parents. He provides knowledge to you through your teachers. He sends blessings to you through elders. In Hindu culture, the elders will always bless you when you approach them. Sometimes they even put their hands on your head as a gesture of blessing (refer to Chapter 10 for a discussion of the Hindu reverence for elders). Worshipping God without first revering one's parents, teachers and elders is impossible, the sages explain. The Taittiriya Upanishad 1.11 thus declares:

"Matri devo bhava."	-	"Let your mother be God."
"Pitri devo bhava."	-	"Let your father be God."
"Āchārya devo bhava."	-	"Let your teacher be God."

Be Respectful of Others

You cannot succeed in life if you don't have good relationships with others around you. Respect is the basis for all human relationships. One of the reasons that the world is in turmoil today is that the sense of respect for one another, for authority, for parents, teachers and others is missing among individuals, families and nations. Everyone seems to do what he (or she) thinks will best serve his interest without giving much thought to how his conduct may affect others.

You must be respectful of others, since respect brings out the best in our relationships with others. Being casual and informal is alright, but you must never step down to the level of overfamiliarity. Familiarity breeds contempt and becoming too familiar is the death of respect.

In English there is only one word "you" to address a person. In many other languages there are two words, one for addressing with respect and the other for addressing with familiarity. In Hindi, we use the word "āp," to express respect and "tum" to express familiarity. Thus being disrespectful to a person is impossible when you address him as "āp." This point may not be appreciated by people who speak only English. Flexibility in language does help to reinforce the awareness of respect and thoughtfulness toward others.

Tradition says that in a person's accomplishments and growth, only parents and teachers are more delighted than the person himself. Regarding respect for guru (teacher), Kabir, a mystic poet of India, once remarked, "When God and guru are both standing at the same place, to whom should I pay my respect first? To the guru, who introduced me to God."

Sexual Freedom is an Illusion

In modern societies uncontrolled sex is called sexual freedom and is considered a splendid trait of the modern civilization. Sages tell us that sex is a sacred activity and must be practiced only in marriage. For this reason, Hindu scriptures hold marriage as a sacrament, and marriage is performed as a religious function in Hindu culture. Hindu culture demands strict celibacy (*Brahmachārya*) before marriage and strict loyalty to the spouse in marriage. Sex outside one's marriage is degrading physically, psychologically, morally and spiritually, and is the source of many social ills, such as teenage pregnancy, abused and neglected children, children with single parents, and children with no parents.

Drugs Destroy the Body and Mind

Drugs do not solve any of our problems or eliminate our worries. They simply alter our consciousness so that we experience temporary relief from the worries or stresses associated with the problems of daily life. At the same time, drugs destroy our bodies and minds and prevent us from leading a normal life. Using drugs to escape from the problems of daily life is akin to choosing to die for a couple of days so that worries cannot touch us as long as we remain dead.

No drug can give long lasting physical and mental relaxation that one can derive from *japa* (repetition of a *mantra* or any Divine name), meditation, yoga exercises, *satsangh* (association with pure and holy persons) and prayers. Do not destroy the mind with drugs—"The human mind is a terrible thing to waste."

Learn to Pray

Prayer is a very powerful tool available to man to purify the mind and gain spiritual strength. Prayer is the foundation of success. Science has not yet recognized the power of prayer. The current attitude of science towards prayer is somewhat the same as Galileo had towards Johannes Kepler's views on gravity. "Galileo condemned Kepler's views as the 'ravings of a madman' when the latter proposed that invisible forces from the moon, acting across gigantic distances, were causing the earth's tides." [27]

In the most carefully controlled scientific study ever performed on the effects of prayer on healing, cardiologist Randolph Byrd, formerly a University of California professor, showed that prayer is a powerful force in healing and that sometimes it can make the difference between life and death for the sick person. [27]

The sages tell us that for a prayer to be effective, faith in the Divine, concentration of the mind, and positive thinking are necessary prerequisites before, during and after the prayer. If one prays for success and at the same time holds thoughts of failure within, the prayer will not be answered. Sages tell us that the mind is the transmitter of prayers. Thus, a prayer transmitted by a restless mind is akin to broadcasting over a broken transmitter. To receive God's answer to our prayers, sages provide the following instructions for prayers:

♦ Meditate before praying to calm restless thoughts. Keep the body still throughout meditation. "Be still and know you are God."

♦ According to yogic literature, the nerve center between the eye-brows (*ajna chakra*) is the transmitter of prayer and the heart is the receiver of God's answer to the prayer. If a prayer is properly transmitted, God's answer appears in the form of subtle feeling(s) arising in the heart following the prayer.

♦ To pray, focus attention at the center between the eyebrows and say the prayer mentally with the deepest devotion of your heart. Repeat the prayer until it becomes one with your consciousness.

♦ Always pray to God as His child, who demands the rightful share of all God's bounties. Never pray to God as a beggar.

♦ Only genuine prayers are fulfilled. "If you pray five hours daily that you might become a Henry Ford, that prayer will not be granted," explains Paramahansa Yogānanda. [23]

Meditate Daily

Meditation provides the ability to silence the mind and experience the inner self. Meditation restores natural power to the mind just as charging restores power to a worn out battery. Meditation destroys worries, fear, and stress that people experience in the "cut-throat" competitive environment of modern societies. When the mind becomes quiet, the body becomes quiet too and knows how to repair itself. The following simple technique may be used to meditate daily:

♦ Sit in a cross-legged pose on the floor or on a chair with feet flat on the ground. Keep the spine straight and fully relax the body and mind. Your overall feeling should be as if you are sitting on the beach of a calm ocean, on a starry cool night of the summer. Close the eyes and gently focus attention at the center between the eyebrows (*ajna chakra*).

♦ Breathe normally (don't force breathing in any way) and say mentally *Rã* (ã as in father) while inhaling and *Mã* (ã as in father) while exhaling. Practice this meditation technique 20 to 30 minutes twice daily, in the mornings and evenings, before meals.

♦ At the end of the meditation, with the eyes closed and attention focused at the center between the eyebrows, say the following prayer, as recommended by Paramahansa Yogānanda:

"I will reason, I will create, I will do everything I set my mind to do, but Oh Lord, guide my creative abilities to do the right thing that I should do." [24]

Chapter 19
Swāmi Vivekānanda's Addresses
at the 1893 World Parliament of Religions

Swami Vivekānanda's addresses at the World Parliament of Religions that opened in Chicago in September, 1893 are invaluable for the clarity and authority with which Swāmiji interpreted the religious and spiritual themes of Hindus for the Western world. Speaking from the depths of his own spiritual experience, which he had attained at the feet of his beloved *guru* (teacher) Paramahamsa Sri Rāmakrishna, Swāmiji distinctly illustrated the essence of the Hindu religious and spiritual tradition in his six addresses at the Parliament of Religions. These addresses are included here from the publication: *Chicago Addresses, Swami Vivekānanda*, with permission from its publisher: Advaita Ashram, Calcutta, India. It is believed that these addresses will help the reader to gain a better understanding of the Hindu religious and spiritual insight.

The World Parliament of Religions was a notable event in mankind's long search for spiritual harmony. Swami Vivekānanda was not an official delegate to the parliament. Nor did he appear at the doors of Chicago with any credentials. He had been sent across the Pacific Ocean by the inspiration of a few of his brother-disciples in Madras. The impelling force, however, that finally drove Swāmi Vivekānanda to the foreign lands was the spiritual genius of Paramahamsa Sri Rāmakrishna, Swāmiji's revered guru.

Thus at the time the World Parliament was to be held in Chicago, Swāmiji happened to be in America. In Boston he met Harvard Professor J. H. Wright, who had attended Swāmiji's talks at a church in Boston. After talking with Swāmiji, Prof. Wright learned that Swāmiji had neither come for the specific purpose of attending the Parliament of Religions at Chicago, nor had he been invited as an official delegate to this world event. A letter of introduction from Prof. Wright—who was himself one of the organizers of the Parliament—that read in part "Here is a man who is more learned than our learned professors put together," enabled Vivekānanda to gain admission and an opportunity to address the Parliament.

The Parliament of Religions opened in Chicago on September 11, 1893. The official delegates represented organized religions professed by the then 1200 million people of the world. The meeting was chaired by Cardinal Gibbons of the Roman Catholic Church. One by one the Chairman called the delegates who read their prepared speeches to the audience of over seven thousand people, who had come from all walks of life and from all over the United States to share the unique experience. When Swami Vivekānanda was called to give his speech, he requested the Chairman to postpone his speech until later. Swāmiji neither had a prepared speech to read from, nor had he any previous experience of addressing such a unique assembly. He was visibly nervous, which he admitted later in the words: "Of course my heart was fluttering and my tongue nearly dried up. I was so nervous that I could not venture to speak in the morning session."

Again Swāmiji was called to give his speech and again he requested a deferment. This happened several times and finally he came to the rostrum and Dr. Barrows introduced him to the audience. Swāmiji bowed to Goddess Saraswatī, the Goddess of learning, and addressed the audience with the historic words, "Sisters and Brothers of America." Upon hearing these five words, thousands in the audience immediately stood up and gave an applause that lasted for over two minutes.

The men and women in the audience were deeply moved to see a man who had discarded the formal words "Ladies and Gentlemen" and had addressed them with the love and warmth of a brother. Although the audience had already heard the theme of universal brotherhood from the earlier speakers, Swāmiji's words reflected spontaneous realization of the spiritual oneness of mankind or unity of existence— the Hindu vision of the world. By addressing the audience as sisters

Chapter 19

and brothers, Swãmiji assured them that each person is a spark of the divine, thus lifting the heavy burden of sin from many a Christian shoulders. After the long applause had subsided, Swãmiji delivered a thundering speech revealing the Hindu spirit of toleration and harmony and the Hindu vision of the cosmic family (*vasudhaiva kutumbakam*).

Miss Harriet Monroe, an American poet, recorded her impression of Swãmiji's performance in these words: "It was the last of these, Swami Vivekãnanda the magnificent, who stole the show and captured the town.....The handsome man in the orange robe gave us, in perfect English, a masterpiece. His personality, dominant, magnetic; his voice rich as a bronze bell; the controlled fervor of his feeling; the beauty of his message to the Western world he was facing for the first time; these combined to give a perfect moment of supreme emotion. It was human eloquence at its highest pitch."

Response to Welcome (9/11/1893)

Sisters and Brothers of America:
It fills my heart with joy unspeakable to rise in response to the warm and cordial welcome which you have given us. I thank you in the name of the most ancient order of monks in the world; I thank you in the name of the mother of religions; and I thank you in the name of the millions and millions of Hindu people of all classes and sects.

My thanks, also, to some of the speakers on this platform who, referring to the delegates from the Orient, have told you that these men from far-off nations may well claim the honor of bearing to different lands the idea of toleration. I am proud to belong to a religion which has taught the world both tolerance and universal acceptance. We believe not only in universal toleration, but we accept all religions as true. I am proud to belong to a nation which has sheltered the persecuted and the refugees of all religions and all nations of the earth. I am proud to tell you that we have gathered in our bosom the purest remnant of the Israelites, who came to southern India and took refuge with us in the very year in which their holy temple was shattered to pieces by Roman tyranny. I am proud to belong to the religion which has sheltered and is still fostering the remnant of the grand Zoroastrian nation. I will quote to you, brethren, a few lines from a hymn which I remember to have repeated from my earliest boyhood, which is every day repeated by millions of human beings: *"As the different streams having their sources in different places all mingle their water in the sea, O Lord, the different paths which men take through different tendencies, various though they appear, crooked or straight, all lead to Thee."*

The present convention, which is one of the most august assemblies ever held, is in itself a vindication, a declaration to the world, of the wonderful doctrine preached in the Gîtâ: *"Whosoever comes to Me through whatsoever form, I reach him; all men are struggling through paths which in the end lead to Me."* Sectarianism, bigotry, and its horrible descendant, fanaticism, have long possessed this beautiful earth. They have filled the earth with violence, drenched it often and often with human blood, destroyed civilization, and sent whole nations to despair. Had it not been for these horrible demons, human society would be far more advanced than it is now.

But their time is come; and I fervently hope that the bell that tolled this morning in honor of this convention may be the death-knell of all fanaticism, of all persecutions with the sword or with the pen, and of all uncharitable feelings between persons wending their way to the same goal.

Why We Disagree (9/15/1893)

I will tell you a little story. You have heard the eloquent speaker who has just finished say, "Let us cease from abusing each other," and he was very sorry that there should be always so much variance.

But I think I should tell you a story which would illustrate the cause of this variance. A frog lived in a well. It had lived there for a long time. It was born there and brought up there, and yet was a little, small frog. Of course, the evolutionists were not there then to tell us whether the frog lost its eyes or not, but, for our story's sake, we must take it for granted that it had its eyes, and that it every day cleansed the water of all the worms and bacilli that lived in it with an energy that would do credit to our modern bacteriologists. In this way it went on and became a little sleek and fat. Well, one day another frog that lived in the sea came and fell into the well.

" Where are you from?"

"I am from the sea."

"The sea! How big is that? Is it as big as my well?"— and he took a leap from one side of the well to the other.

"My friend," said the frog of the sea, "how do you compare the sea with your little well?"

Then the frog took another leap and asked, "Is your sea so big?"

"What nonsense you speak, to compare the sea with your well!"

"Well, then, said the frog of the well, "nothing can be bigger than my well; there can be nothing bigger than this; this fellow is a liar, so turn him out."

That has been the difficulty all the while. I am a Hindu. I am sitting in my own little well and thinking that the whole world is my little well. The Christian sits in his little well and thinks the whole world is his well. The Mohammedan sits in his little well and thinks that is the whole world. I have to thank you of America for the great attempt you are making to break down the barriers of this little world of ours, and hope that, in the future, the Lord will help you to accomplish your purpose.

Paper on Hinduism (9/19/1893)

Three religions now stand in the world which have come down to us from time prehistoric - Hinduism, Zoroastrianism, and Judaism. They have all received tremendous shocks, and all of them prove by their survival their internal strength. But while Judaism failed to absorb Christianity and was driven out of its place of birth by its all-conquering daughter, and a handful of Parsees is all that remains to tell the tale of their grand religion, sect after sect arose in India and seemed to shake the religion of the Vedas to its very foundations, but like the waters of the sea-shore in a tremendous earthquake it receded only for a while, only to return in an all-absorbing flood, a thousand times more vigorous, and when the tumult of the rush was over, these sects were all sucked in, absorbed and assimilated into the immense body of the mother faith.

From the high spiritual flights of the Vedanta philosophy, of which the latest discoveries of science seem like echoes, to the low ideas of idolatry with its multifarious mythology, the agnosticism of the Buddhists and the atheism of the Jains, each and all have a place in the Hindu's religion.

Where then, the question arises, where is the common center to which all these widely diverging radii converge? Where is the common basis upon which all these seemingly hopeless contradictions rest? And this is the question I shall attempt to answer.

The Hindus have received their religion through revelation, the Vedas. They hold that the Vedas are without beginning and without end. It may sound ludicrous to this audience, how a book can be without beginning or end. But by the Vedas no books are meant. They mean the accumulated treasury of spiritual laws discovered by different persons in different times.

Chapter 19

Just as the law of gravitation existed before its discovery, and would exist if all humanity forgot it, so is it with the laws that govern the spiritual world. The moral, ethical and spiritual relations between soul and soul and between individual spirits and the Father of all spirits were there before their discovery, and would remain even if we forgot them.

The discoverers of these laws are called *Rishis*, and we honor them as perfected beings. I am glad to tell this audience that some of the very greatest of them were women.

Here it may be said that these laws as laws may be without end, but they must have had a beginning. The Vedas teach us that creation is without beginning or end. Science is said to have proved that the sum total of cosmic energy is always the same. Then, if there was a time when nothing existed, where was all this manifested energy? Some say it was in a potential form in God. In that case God is sometimes potential and sometimes kinetic, which would make Him mutable. Everything mutable is a compound, and everything compound must undergo that change which is called destruction. So God would die, which is absurd. Therefore there never was a time when there was no creation.

If I may be allowed to use simile, creation and creator are two lines, without beginning and without end, running parallel to each other. God is the ever-active providence, by whose power systems after systems are being evolved out of chaos, made to run for a time, and again destroyed. This is what the Brahmin boy repeats every day: *"The sun and the moon, the Lord created like the suns and moons of previous cycles."* And this agrees with modern science.

Here I stand and if I shut my eyes, and try to conceive my existence, "I," "I," "I," what is the idea before me? The idea of a body. Am I, then, nothing but a combination of material substances? The Vedas declare, "No." I am a spirit living in a body. I am not the body. The body will die, but I shall not die. Here am I in this body; it will fall, but I shall go on living. I had also a past. The soul was not created, for creation means a combination, which means a certain future dissolution. If then the soul was created, it must die. Some are born happy, enjoy perfect health with beautiful body, mental vigor, and all wants supplied. Others are born miserable; some are without hands or feet; others again are idiots, and only drag on a wretched existence. Why, if they are all created, why does a just and merciful God create one happy and another unhappy, why is He so partial? Nor would it mend matters in the least to hold that those who are

Chapter 19

miserable in this life will be happy in a future one. Why should a man be miserable even here in the reign of a just and merciful God?

In the second place, the idea of a creator God does not explain the anomaly, but simply expresses the cruel fiat of an all-powerful being. There must have been causes, then, before his birth, to make a man miserable or happy and those were his past actions.

Are not all the tendencies of the mind and the body accounted for by inherited aptitude? Here are two parallel lines of existence—one of the mind, the other of matter. If matter and its transformations answer for all that we have, there is no necessity for supposing the existence of a soul. But it cannot be proved that thought has been evolved out of matter; and if a philosophical [intellectual] monism is inevitable, spiritual monism is certainly logical and no less desirable than a materialistic monism; but neither of these is necessary here.

We cannot deny that bodies acquire certain tendencies from heredity, but those tendencies only mean the physical configuration through which a peculiar mind alone can act in a peculiar way. There are other tendencies peculiar to a soul caused by his past actions. And a soul with a certain tendency would, by the laws of affinity, take birth in a body which is the fittest instrument for the display of that tendency. This is in accord with science, for science wants to explain everything by habit, and habit is got through repetitions. So repetitions are necessary to explain the natural habits of a newborn soul. And since they were not obtained in this present life, they must have come down from past lives.

There is another suggestion. Taking all these for granted, how is it that I do not remember anything of my past life? This can be easily explained. I am now speaking English. It is not my mother tongue; in fact, no words of my mother tongue are now present in my consciousness; but let me try to bring them up, and they rush in. That shows that consciousness is only the surface of the mental ocean, and within its depths are stored up all our experiences. Try and struggle, they would come up, and you would be conscious even of your past life.

This is direct and demonstrative evidence. Verification is the perfect proof of a theory, and here is the challenge thrown to the world by the *Rishis*. We have discovered the secret by which the very depths of the ocean of memory can be stirred up. Try it and you would get a complete reminiscence of your past life.

So then the Hindu believes that he is a spirit. Him the sword cannot pierce, him the fire cannot burn, him the water cannot melt, him the air

Chapter 19

cannot dry.   The Hindu believes that every soul is a circle whose circumference is nowhere but whose center is located in the body, and that death means the change of this center from body to body. Nor is the soul bound by the conditions of matter.   In its very essence, it is free, unbounded, holy, pure, and perfect. But somehow or other it finds itself tied down to matter, and thinks of itself as matter.

Why should the free, perfect and pure being be thus under the thralldom of matter, is the next question. How can the perfect soul be deluded into the belief that it is imperfect? We have been told that the Hindus shirk the question and say that no such question can be there. Some thinkers want to answer it by positing one or more quasi-perfect beings, and use big scientific names to fill up the gap. But naming is not explaining. How can the perfect become the quasi-perfect; how can the pure, the absolute change even a microscopic particle of its nature? But the Hindu is sincere. He does not want to take shelter under sophistry. He is brave enough to face the question in a manly fashion; and his answer is: "I do not know. I do not know how the perfect being, the soul, came to think of itself as imperfect, as joined to and conditioned by matter." But the fact is a fact for all that.   It is a fact in everybody's consciousness that one thinks of oneself as the body. The Hindu does not attempt to explain why one thinks one is the body. The answer that it is the will of God is no explanation. This is nothing more than what the Hindu says, "I don't know."

Well, then, the human soul is eternal and immortal, perfect and infinite, and death means only a change of center from one body to another. The present is determined by our past actions, and the future by the present. The soul will go on evolving up or reverting back from birth to birth and death to death. But here is another question: Is man a tiny boat in a tempest, raised one moment on the foamy crest of a billow and dashed down into a yawning chasm the next, rolling to and fro at the mercy of good and bad actions—a powerless, helpless wreck in an ever-raging, ever-rushing, uncompromising current of cause and effect—a little moth placed under the wheel of causation, which rolls on crushing everything in its way and waits not for the widow's tears or the orphan's cry? The heart sinks at the idea, yet this is the law of nature. Is there no hope? Is there no escape?   The cry that went up from the bottom of the heart of despair, reached the throne of mercy, and words of hope and consolation came down and inspired a Vedic sage, and he stood up before the world and in trumpet voice proclaimed the glad tidings: "Hear, ye children of immortal

Chapter 19

bliss! I have found the Ancient One who is beyond all darkness, all delusion; knowing Him alone you shall be saved from death over again." "Children of immortal bliss"—what a sweet, what a hopeful name! Allow me to call you, brethren, by that sweet name—heirs of immortal bliss. Yea, the Hindu refuses to call you sinners. We are the Children of God, the sharers of immortal bliss, holy and perfect beings. Ye divinities on earth—sinners! It is a sin to call a man so; it is standing libel on human nature. Come up, O lions, and shake off the delusion that you are sheep; you are souls immortal, spirits free, blest and eternal; ye are not matter, ye are not bodies; matter is your servant, not you the servant of matter.

Thus it is that the Vedas proclaim not a dreadful combination of unforgiving laws, not an endless prison of cause and effect, but that at the head of all these laws, in and through every particle of matter and force, stands One, "by whose command the wind blows, the fire burns, the clouds rain, and death stalks upon the earth".

And what is His nature?

He is everywhere, the pure and formless One, the Almighty and the All-merciful. "Thou art our father, Thou art our mother, Thou art our beloved friend. Thou art the source of all strength; give us strength. *Thou art He that beareth the burdens of the universe*; help me bear the little burden of this life." Thus sang the Rishis of the Veda. And how to worship Him? Through love. "He is to be worshipped as the one beloved, dearer than everything in this and the next life."

This is the doctrine of love declared, developed and taught by Krishna whom the Hindu believe to have been God incarnate on earth.

He taught that a man ought to live in this world like a lotus leaf, which grows in water but is never moistened by water; so a man ought to live in the world—his heart to God and his hands to work.

It is good to love God for hope of reward in this or the next world, but it is better to love God for love's sake; and the prayer goes: "Lord, I do not want wealth nor children nor learning. If it be Thy will, I shall go from birth to birth; but grant me this, that I may love Thee without the hope of reward—love unselfishly for love's sake." One of the disciples of Krishna, the then Emperor of India, was driven from his kingdom by his enemies and had to take shelter with his queen, in a forest in the Himalayas and there one day the queen asked him how it was that he, the most virtuous of men, should suffer so much misery. Yudhishthira answered, "Behold, my queen, the Himalayas, how grand and beautiful they are; I love them. They do not give me anything but my nature is to love the grand, the beautiful,

therefore I love them. Similarly, I love the Lord. He is the source of all
beauty, of all sublimity. He is the only object to be loved; my nature is to
love Him, and therefore I love. I do not pray for anything; I do not ask for
anything. Let Him place me wherever He likes. I must love Him for love's
sake. I cannot trade in love."

The Vedas teach that the soul is divine, only held in the bondage of
matter; perfection will be reached when this bond will burst, and the word
they use for it is, therefore, Mukti—freedom, freedom from the bonds of
imperfection, freedom from death and misery.

And this bondage can only fall off through the mercy of God, and this
mercy comes on the pure. So purity is the condition of His mercy. How
does that mercy act? He reveals Himself to the pure heart; the pure and the
stainless see God, yea, even in this life; then and then only all the
crookedness of the heart is made straight. Then all doubt ceases. He is no
more the freak of a terrible law of causation. This is the very center, the
very vital conception or Hinduism. The Hindu does not want to live upon
words and theories. If there are existences beyond the ordinary sensuous
existence, he wants to come face to face with them. If there is a soul in
him which is not matter, if there is an all-merciful universal Soul, he will
go to Him direct. He must see Him, and that alone can destroy all doubts.
So the best proof a Hindu sage gives about the soul, about God, is: "I have
seen the soul; I have seen God." And that Hindu religion does not consist
in struggles and attempts to believe a certain doctrine or dogma, but in
realizing—not in believing, but in being and becoming.

Thus the whole object of their system is by constant struggle to become
perfect, to become divine, to reach God, and see God; and this reaching
God, seeing God, becoming perfect even as the Father in Heaven is perfect,
constitutes the religion of the Hindus.

And what becomes of a man when he attains perfection? He lives a
life of bliss infinite. He enjoys infinite and perfect bliss, having obtained
the only thing in which man ought to have pleasure, namely God, and
enjoys the bliss with God.

So far all the Hindus are agreed. This is the common religion of all
the sects of India; but then perfection is absolute, and the absolute cannot
be two or three. It cannot have any qualities. It cannot be an individual.
And so when a soul becomes perfect and absolute, it must become one with
Brahman, and it would only realize the Lord as the perfection, the reality,
of its own nature and existence, the existence absolute, knowledge absolute,

and bliss absolute. We have often and often read this called the losing of individuality and becoming a stock or a stone.

"He jests at scars that never felt a wound."

I tell you it is nothing of the kind. If it is happiness to enjoy the consciousness of this small body, it must be greater happiness to enjoy the consciousness of two bodies, the measure of happiness increasing with the consciousness of an increasing number of bodies, the aim, the ultimate of happiness, being reached when it would become a universal consciousness.

Therefore, to gain this infinite universal individuality, this miserable little prison-individuality must go. Then alone can death cease when I am one with life, then alone can misery cease when I am one with happiness itself, then alone can all errors cease when I am one with knowledge itself; and this is the necessary scientific conclusion. Science has proved to me that physical individuality is a delusion, that really my body is one little continuously changing body in an unbroken ocean of matter, and Advaita (unity) is the necessary conclusion with my other counterpart, Soul.

Science is nothing but the finding of unity. As soon as science would reach perfect unity, it would stop from further progress, because it would reach the goal. Thus chemistry could not progress farther when it would discover one element out of which all others could be made. Physics would stop when it would be able to fulfill its services in discovering one energy of which all the others are but manifestations, and the science of religion becomes perfect when it would discover Him who is the one life in a universe of death, Him who is the constant basis of an ever-changing world, One who is the only Soul of which all souls are but delusive manifestations. Thus is it, through multiplicity and duality, that the ultimate unity is reached. Religion can go no farther. This is the goal of all science.

All science is bound to come to this conclusion in the long run. Manifestation, and not creation, is the word of science today; and the Hindu is only glad that what he has been cherishing in his bosom for ages is going to be taught in more forcible language and with further light from the latest conclusions of science.

Descend we now from the aspirations of philosophy to the religion of the ignorant. At the very outset, I may tell you that there is no *polytheism* in India. In every temple, if one stands by and listens, one will find the worshippers applying all the attributes of God, including omnipresence, to the images. It is not polytheism, nor would the name henotheism explain the situation.

Chapter 19

"The rose, called by any other name, would smell as sweet." Names are not explanations.

I remember, as a boy, hearing a Christian missionary preach to a crowd in India. Among other sweet things he was telling them was, that if he gave a blow to their idol with his stick, what could it do? One of his hearers sharply answered, "If I abuse your God, what can He do?" "You would be punished," said the preacher, "when you die." "So my idol will punish you when you die," retorted the Hindu.

The tree is known by its fruits. When I have seen amongst them that are called idolaters, men, the like of whom, in morality and spirituality and love, I have never seen anywhere, I stop and ask myself, "Can sin beget holiness?"

Superstition is a great enemy of man, but bigotry is worse. Why does a Christian go to church? Why is the cross holy? Why is the face turned toward the sky in prayer? Why are there so many images in the Catholic Church? Why are there so many images in the minds of Protestants when they pray? My brethren, we can no more think about anything without a mental image than we can live without breathing. By the law of association the material image calls up the mental idea and vice versa. This is why the Hindu uses an external symbol when he worships. He will tell you, it helps to keep his mind fixed on the Being to whom he prays. He knows as well as you do that the image in not God, is not omnipresent. After all, how much does omnipresence mean to almost the whole world? It stands merely as a word, a symbol. Has God superficial area? If not, when we repeat that word "omnipresent", we think of the extended sky, or of space - that is all.

As we find that somehow or other, by the laws of our mental constitution, we have to associate our ideas of infinity with the image of the blue sky, or of the sea, so we naturally connect our idea of holiness with the image of a church, a mosque, or a cross. The Hindus have associated the ideas of holiness, purity, truth, omnipresence, and such other ideas with different images and forms. But with this difference that while some people devote their whole lives to their idol of a church and never rise higher, because with them religion means an intellectual assent to certain doctrines and doing good to their fellows, the whole religion of the Hindu is centered in realization. Man is to become divine by realizing the divine. Idols or temples or churches or books are only the supports, the helps, of his spiritual childhood; but on and on he must progress.

Chapter 19

He must not stop anywhere. *"External worship, material worship,"* say the scriptures, *"is the lowest stage; struggling to rise high, mental prayer is the next stage, but the highest stage is when the Lord has been realized."* Mark, the same earnest man who is kneeling before the idol tell you, *"Him the sun cannot express, nor the moon, nor the stars, the lightning cannot express Him, nor what we speak of as fire; through Him they shine."* But he does not abuse any one's idol or call its worship sin. He recognizes in it a necessary stage of life. *"The child is father of the man."* Would it be right for an old man to say that childhood is a sin or youth a sin?

If a man can realize his divine nature with the help of an image, would it be right to call that a sin? Nor, even when he has passed that stage, should he call it an error. To the Hindu, man is not traveling from error to truth, but from truth to truth, from lower to higher truth. To him all the religions, from the lowest fetishism to the highest absolutism, mean so many attempts of the human soul to grasp and realize the Infinite, each determined by the conditions of its birth and association, and each of these marks a stage of progress; and every soul is a young eagle soaring higher and higher, gathering more and more strength till it reaches the glorious sun.

Unity in variety is the plan of nature, and the Hindu has recognized it Every other religion lays down certain fixed dogmas and tries to force society to adopt them. It places before society only one coat which must fit Jack and John and Henry, all alike. If it does not fit John or Henry, he must go without a coat to cover his body. The Hindus have discovered that the absolute can only be realized, or thought of, or stated through the relative, and the images, crosses and crescents are simply so many symbols - so many pegs to hang spiritual ideas on. It is not that this help is necessary for everyone, but those that do not need it have no right to say that it is wrong. Nor is it compulsory in Hinduism.

One thing I must tell you. Idolatry in India does not mean anything horrible. It is not the mother of harlots. On the other hand, it is the attempt of undeveloped minds to grasp high spiritual truths. The Hindus have their faults, they sometimes have their exceptions; but mark this, they are always for punishing their own bodies, and never for cutting the throats of their neighbors. If the Hindu fanatic burns himself on the pyre, he never lights the fire of Inquisition. And even this cannot be laid at the door of his religion any more than the burning of witches can be laid at the door of Christianity.

Chapter 19

To the Hindu, then, the whole world of religions is only a traveling, a coming up, of different men and women, through various conditions and circumstances, to the same goal. Every religion is only evolving a God out of the material man, and the same God is the inspirer of all of them. Why, then, are there so many contradictions? They are only apparent, says the Hindu. The contradictions come from the same truth adapting itself to the varying circumstances of different natures.

It is the same light coming through the glasses of different colors. And these little variations are necessary for purposes of adaptation. But in the heart of everything the same truth reigns. The Lord has declared to the Hindu in His incarnation as Krishna: *"I am in every religion as the thread through a string of pearls. Wherever thou seest extraordinary holiness and extraordinary power raising and purifying humanity, know thou that I am there."* And what has been the result? I challenge the world to find, throughout the whole system of Sanskrit philosophy, any such expression as that the Hindu alone will be saved and not others. Says Vyasa, "We find perfect men even beyond the pale of our caste and creed." One thing more. How, then, can the Hindu, whose whole fabric of thought centers in God, believe in Buddhism which is agnostic, or in Jainism which is atheistic?

The Buddhists or Jains do not depend upon God; but the whole force of their religion is directed to the great central truth in every religion, to evolve a God out of man. They have not seen the Father, but they have seen the Son. And *"he that hath seen the Son hath seen the Father also."*

This, brethren, is a short sketch of the religious ideas of the Hindus. The Hindu may have failed to carry out all his plans, but if there is ever to be a universal religion, it must be one which will have no location in place or time; which will be infinite like the God it will preach, and whose sun will shine upon the followers of Krishna and Christ, on saints and sinners alike; which will not be Brahmanic or Buddhistic, Christian or Mohammedan, but the sum total of all these, and still have infinite space for development; which in its catholicity will embrace in infinite arms, and find a place for, every human being from the lowest groveling savage, not far removed from the brute, to the highest man towering by the virtues of his head and heart almost above humanity, making society stand in awe of him and doubt his human nature. It will be a religion which will have no place for prosecution or intolerance in its polity, which will recognize divinity in every man and woman, and whose whole scope, whose whole force, will be centered in aiding humanity to realize its own true, divine nature.

Offer such religion and all the nations will follow you. Ashoka's council was a council of the Buddhist faith. Akbar's, though more to the purpose, was only a parlor meeting. It was reserved for America to proclaim to all quarters of the globe that the Lord is in every religion.

May He who is the Brahman of the Hindu, the Ahura-Mazda of the Zoroastrians, the Buddha of the Buddhists, the Jehovah of the Jews, the Father in Heaven of the Christians, give strength to you to carry out your noble ideal! The star arose in the East; it traveled steadily towards the West, sometimes dimmed and sometimes effulgent, till it made a circuit of the world, and now it is again rising on the very horizon of the East, the borders of the Sanpo (see Note), a thousandfold more effulgent than it ever was before.

Hail Columbia, motherland of liberty! It has given to thee, who never dipped her hand in her neighbor's blood, who never found out that the shortest way of becoming rich was by robbing one's neighbors, it has been given to thee to march at the vanguard of civilization with the flag of harmony.

Note: Sanpo is a Tibetan name for the Brahamaputra River, India. According to *the World's Parliament of Religions* (Chicago: The Parliament Publishing Company, 1893), Vol. II, pp. 978, the word is "Tasifu." Marie Louise Burke in her book *Swami Vivekānanda in the West: New Discoveries: His Prophetic Mission* (Mayavati: Advaita Ashram, 1983), Vol. I, pp. 143-44, opines that the word should be "Pacific."

Religion is Not the Crying Need for India (9/20/1893)

Christians must always be ready for good criticism and I hardly think that you will mind if I make a little criticism. You Christians, who are so fond of sending out missionaries to save the soul of the heathen—why do you not try to save their bodies from starvation? In India, during the terrible famines, thousands died from hunger, yet you Christians did nothing. You erect churches all through India, but the crying evil in the East is not religion—they have religion enough—but it is the bread that the suffering millions of burning India cry out for with parched throats. They ask us for bread, but we give them stones [churches]. It is an insult to starving people to offer them religion; it is an insult to a starving man to teach him metaphysics. In India a priest that preached for money would lose cast and be spat upon by the people. I came here to seek aid for my impoverished people, and I fully realized how difficult it was to get help for heathens from Christians in a Christian land.

Buddhism, the Fulfillment of Hinduism (9/26/93)

I am not a Buddhist, as you have heard, and yet I am. If China, or Japan, or Ceylon follow the teachings of the Great Master, India worships him as God incarnate on earth. You have just now heard that I am going to criticize Buddhism, but by that I wish you to understand only this. Far be it from me to criticize him who I worship as God incarnate on earth. But our views about Buddha are that he was not understood properly by his disciples. The relation between Hinduism (by Hinduism, I mean the religion of the Vedas) and what is called Buddhism at the present day, is nearly the same as between Judaism and Christianity. Jesus Christ was a Jew, and Shakya Muni was a Hindu. The Jews rejected Jesus Christ, nay, crucified him, and the Hindus have accepted Shakya Muni as God and worship him. But the real difference that we Hindus want to show between modern Buddhism and what we should understand as the teachings of Lord Buddha, lies principally in this: Shakya Muni came to preach nothing new. He also, like Jesus, came to fulfill and not to destroy. Only, in the case of Jesus, it was the old people, the Jews, who did not understand him, while in the case of Buddha, it was his own followers who did not realize the import of his teachings. As the Jew did not understand the fulfillment of the Old Testament, so the Buddhist did not understand the fulfillment of the truths of the Hindu religion. Again, I repeat, Shakya Muni came not to destroy, but he was the fulfillment, the logical conclusion, the logical development of the religion of the Hindus.

The religion of the Hindus is divided into two parts, the ceremonial and the spiritual; the spiritual portion is specially studied by the monks. In that there is no caste. A man from the highest caste and a man from the lowest caste become a monk in India and the two castes become equal. In religion there is no caste; caste is simply a social institution. Shakya Muni himself was a monk, and it was his glory that he had the large-heartedness to bring out the truths from the hidden Vedas and throw them broadcast all over the world. He was the first being who brought missionarizing into practice—nay, he was the first to conceive the idea of proselytizing.

Chapter 19

The great glory of the Master lay in his wonderful sympathy for everybody, especially for the ignorant and the poor. Some of his disciples were Brahmins. When Buddha was teaching, Sanskrit was no more the spoken language in India. It was then only in the books of the learned. Some of Buddha's Brahmin disciples wanted to translate his teachings into Sanskrit, but he distinctly told them, "I am for the poor, for the people: let me speak in the language of the people." And so to this day the great bulk of his teachings are in the vernacular of the day in India.

Whatever may be the position of the philosophy, whatever may be the position of the metaphysics, so long as there is such a thing as death in the world, so long as there is such a thing as weakness in the human heart, so long as there is a cry going out of the heart of man in his very weakness, there shall be a faith in God.

On the philosophic side, the disciples of the Great Master dashed themselves against the eternal rocks of the Vedas and could not crush them, and on the other side they took away from the nation that eternal God to which everyone, man or woman, clings so fondly. And the result was that Buddhism had to die a natural death in India. At the present day there is not one who calls himself Buddhist in India, the land of its birth.

But at the same time, Brahminism lost something—that reforming zeal, that wonderful sympathy and charity for everybody, that wonderful leaven which Buddhism had brought to the masses and which had rendered Indian society so great that a Greek historian who wrote about India of that time was led to say that no Hindu was known to tell an untruth and no Hindu woman was known to be unchaste.

Hinduism cannot live without Buddhism, nor Buddhism without Hinduism. Then realize what the separation has shown to us, that the Buddhist cannot stand without the brain and philosophy of the Brahmins, nor the Brahmin without the heart of the Buddhist. This separation between the Buddhist and the Brahmin is the cause of the downfall of India. That is why India is populated by three hundred millions of beggars, and that is why India has been the slave of conquerors for the last thousand years. Let us then join the wonderful intellect of the Brahmin with the heart, the noble soul, the wonderful humanizing power of the Great Master.

Chapter 19

Address at the Final Session (9/27/1893)

The World's Parliament of Religions has become an accomplished fact, and the merciful Father has helped those who labored to bring it into existence, and crowned with success their most unselfish labor.

My thanks to those noble souls whose large hearts and love of truth first dreamed this wonderful dream and then realized it. My thanks to the shower of liberal sentiments that has overflowed this platform. My thanks to this enlightened audience for their uniform kindness to me and for their appreciation of every thought that tends to smooth the friction of religions. A few jarring notes were heard from time to time in this harmony. My special thanks to them, for they have, by their striking contrast, made the general harmony sweeter.

Much has been said of the common ground of religious unity. I am not just now going to venture my own theory. But if anyone here hopes that this unity will come by the triumph of any one of the religions and the destruction of the others, to him I say, "Brother, yours is an impossible hope." Do I wish that the Christian would become Hindu? God forbid. Do I wish that the Hindu or Buddhist would become Christian? God forbid.

The seed is put in the ground, and earth and air and water are placed around it. Does the seed become the earth, or the air, or the water? No. It becomes a plant, it develops after the law of its own growth, assimilates the air, the earth, and the water, converts them into plant substance, and grows into a plant.

Similar is the case with religion. The Christian is not to become a Hindu or a Buddhist, nor a Hindu or a Buddhist to become a Christian. But each must assimilate the spirit of the others and yet preserve his individuality and grow according to his own law of growth.

If the Parliament of Religions has shown anything to the world it is this: It has proved to the world that holiness, purity and charity are not the exclusive possessions of any church in the world, and that every system has produced men and women of the most exalted character. In the face of this evidence, if anybody dreams of the exclusive survival of his own religion and the destruction of others, I pity him from the bottom of my heart, and point out to him that upon the banner of every religion will soon be written, in spite of resistance: "Help and not fight," "Assimilation and not Destruction," "Harmony and Peace and not Dissension."

Chapter 19

Works Cited

1. Subramuniyaswāmi, Satguru Sivaya. *Dancing With Shiva: Hinduism's Contemporary Catechism.* Hawaii: Himalayan Academy, 1993.

2. Kapur, K. N. "Age of Mahābhārata War." *Vedic Light,* April, 1981. New Delhi, India.

3. *Rig Veda* 1.164.46 (mandala 1, hymn 164, mantra 46).

4. *Sukla Yajur Veda Brihadāranyaka Upanishad* 1.3.28.

5. Rādhākrishnan, S. *Eastern Religions and Western Thought.* London: Oxford University Press, 1949. pp. 336-337.

6. Ibid. pp. 310-311.

7. *Mahābhārata Shāntiparva* 262.5-6.

8. *Manu Samhitā* II.1, 6, 12.

9. *Mahābhārata Āpadharmaparva* 140-143.

10. *Young India,* April 24, 1924—a weekly journal edited by Mahatma Gandhi; ceased publication in February 1932.

11. *Krishna Yajur Veda Svetasvatara Upanishad* 3.20.

12. Swāhananda, Swāmî, trans. *Chāndogya Upanishad.* Madras, India: Sri Rāmakrishna Math, 1956.

13. Heimann, Betty. *Facets of Indian Thought.* New York: Schocken Books, 1964.

14. *Chāndogya Upanishad* 3.14.1.

15. *Young India,* September 11, 1924— ceased publication in Feb., 1932

16. Satchidānanda, Swāmî, trans. *The Yoga Sutras of Patānjali.* Buckingam, Virginia: Integral Yoga Publications.

17. Toynbee, A. J. *A study of History.* New York: Oxford University Press, 1951. p. 501.

18. *Harijan,* July 20, 1935—a weekly journal edited by Mahatma Gandhi and others and published at Ahmedabad, India.

19. Prime, Ranchor. *Hinduism and Ecology.* Delhi, India: Motilal Banarsidas, 1994.

20. *Manu Samhitā* 7.2.

21. Mascaro, Juan, trans. *The Bhagavad Gîtā.* New York: Penguin Books, 1962. p. 9.

22. Bishop, Donald H., ed. "Epilogue." *Indian Thought.* New York: John Wiley and Sons. p. 383.

23. Howe, Quincy. "Rethinking the Religious Life." *Self-Realization: A Magazine Devoted to Healing of Body, Mind and Soul,* Spring 1996. Los Angeles: Self-Realization Fellowship.

24. Yogānanda, Paramahansa. *Scientific Healing Affirmations.* Los Angeles: Self-Realization Fellowship.

25. Aiyer, Ramaswami C.P. "The Philosophical Basis of Indian Legal and Social Systems." *The Indian Mind.* Moore, Charles A., ed. Honolulu: University of Hawaii Press, 1967. p. 262.

26. Madison, Dorothy and Ann Myren, eds. *Living at the Source: Yoga Teachings of Vivekānanda.* Boston: Shambhala, 1993. pp. 100-101.

27. Dossey, Larry. "The Power of Prayers." *Self-Realization: A Magazine Devoted to Healing of Body, Mind and Soul.* Los Angeles: Self-Realization Fellowship.

28. Ifrah, Georges. *From One to Zero: A Universal History of Numbers.* New York: Viking Penguin Inc., 1985. pp. 458-464.

29. Jyotirmayananda, Swāmî. *Advice to Students.* South Miami, Florida: Yoga Research Foundation. p. 207.

30. *Thus Spake Vivekānanda.* Madras, India: Sri Rāmakrishna Math.

31. Lukes, Alan and Peggy Payne. *The Healing Power of Doing Good.* New York: Fawcell, 1991.

32. Pandit, Bansi. *The Hindu Mind: Fundamentals of Hindu Religion and Philosophy for All Ages,* Second Edition. Glen Ellyn, Illinois: B & V Enterprises, 1996. pp. 74-75 and 291-300.

Subject Index

OTHER BOOK BY THE SAME AUTHOR:
The Hindu Mind
Fundamentals of Hindu Religion
and Philosophy for All Ages
(432 pages, soft cover, ISBN 0-9634798-1-4)
(432 pages, hard cover, ISBN 0-9634798-2-2)